# The MYSTERY FANcier

Volume 4   Number 3
May/June   1980

# THE MYSTERY FANCIER

Volume 4 Number 3
May/June 1980

## TABLE OF CONTENTS

MYSTERIOUSLY SPEAKING . . . . . . . . . . . . . . . . . . . . 1
The Nero Wolfe Saga, Part XIX, by Guy M. Townsend . . . . . 3
Vladimir Gull, by Theodore P. Dukeshire . . . . . . . . . . 22
Spy Series Characters in Hardback, Part II, by
  Barry Van Tilburg . . . . . . . . . . . . . . . . . . . . 23
Looking for Rachel Wallace and Ginger North, by
  George Kelley . . . . . . . . . . . . . . . . . . . . . . 29
IT'S ABOUT CRIME, by Marvin Lachman . . . . . . . . . . . . 31
MYSTERY*FILE: Short Reviews by Steve Lewis . . . . . . . . 34
VERDICTS (More Reviews) . . . . . . . . . . . . . . . . . . 42
THE DOCUMENTS IN THE CASE (Letters) . . . . . . . . . . . . 47

*The MYSTERY FANcier*
*(USPS:428-590)*
is edited and published bi-monthly by Guy M. Townsend,
2245 Shawnee Dr. #1, Madison, Indiana 47250, U.S.A.
Contributions of all descriptions are welcomed.

SUBSCRIPTION RATES: Domestic second class mail, $9.00 per year (6 issues); Overseas surface mail, $9.00; Overseas airmail, $12.00. Overseas subscribers please pay in international money order, check drawn on U.S. bank, or currency; no checks drawn of foreign banks, please.

Second class postage paid at Madison, Indiana

Copyright 1980 by Guy M. Townsend
All rights reserved for contributors
ISSN:0146-3160

# MYSTERIOUSLY SPEAKING...

Surprise, everybody—I've got a new address! Actually, it's only a temporary address until I find a house to live in. I am, you see, going back to Arkansas just as soon as I get this issue in the mail to you folks. I don't yet know what my home address will be, so I ask that you address any response to this issue (and all other contributions) to me, care of the Courier News, Broadway and Moultrie, Blytheville, AR 72315. I'll have to get the second class mailing permit changed over (again), and next time I'll give you a new permanent address. As permanent, that is, as these addresses ever seem to be for me. If you folks think it's tough keeping up with all my address changes, just imagine how tough it is on me to have to make them.

Last issue I had to recycle a cover, but this time Bob Napier came through with another one in time. Thanks, Bob. I need more, folks.

In the good news department, it is my pleasure (and relief) to announce that the Rex Stout bibliography, on which John McAleer, Jud Sapp, Arriean Schemer, and I have been working off and on for nearly two years now, is finally completed. I am proofing the final manuscript now and preparing the index. The whole thing will be in the hands of the publisher (Garland) by the first of August, and Garland has promised to have the book ready in time for the annual Nero Wolfe gathering in New York early in December. Otto Penzler is planning to hold an autograph party for us at his Mysterious Bookshop on the same weekend. John and Jud will be there for sure, and it looks as though I'll be able to make it, too. Don't know yet if Arriean will be there, but three out of four ain't bad, you know. The book is completely annotated (except for Stout's poetry and a dozen or so pastiches, which are merely listed) and runs to more than 200 pages. Garland hasn't said yet, but, judging from its prices for comparable books, it ought to sell for $20 or $25.

I am also pleased to mention that Steve Stilwell's index to the first ten years of TAD is now available from *The Armchair Detective*, 129 W. 56th St., New York, NY 10019, for $7.50. Officially, the title is *The Armchair Detective Index (Volumes 1-10, 1967-1977)*, compiled by Steven A. Stilwell. In his brief "Introduction and User's guide" Steve explains that "This is an alphabetical index by author, title, and subject to all of the articles, reviews and letters which have appeared in *The Armchair Detective* between October 1967 and October 1977. The First Ten Years." Anyone who has tried to locate a piece in TAD by memory will not have to be told just how useful a tool this book is. Admittedly, the number of those of us who are lucky enough to possess a complete run of TAD is limited, but even newcomers will find the book useful in locating pieces in the issues they do have, as well as for interesting themselves in the issues they don't have. For instance, how can you possibly live without knowing what Mike Nevins had to say in his article in volume one entitled "The Worst Legal Mystery in the World"? Buy this book; a lot of your friends (and enimies) are in it.

Another book I should draw your attention to is *Twentieth Century Crime and Mystery Writers*, edited by John M. Reilly and available from St. Martin's Press for a mere $50.00.

1

Which really isn't bad, when you consider that the book (7x9½) has 1600 pages and covers over 600 writers. Each entry consists of "a carefully researched short biography; a complete booklist, including uncollected short stories; details of the author's published bibliography, if one exists; a short, signed critical essay; in many cases, a comment by the author on his or her own work." John Reilly is a TMFer, and the book's advisory board includes these familiar names, all of whom are in our family: Jane S. Bakerman, E. F. Bleiler, Jon L. Breen, George N. Dove, Allen J. Hubin, Francis M. Nevins, Jr., and Donald B. Yates. At a guess I would say that a good two dozen or more TMFers contributed one or more article to the book (I can't say for sure since my copy, though ordered, has not yet arrived), so you'll find many familiar names therein beside the authors the book is about.

And there's another book that I just have to mention. Some might call it a book catalogue, but I call it a book, period. The names Gravesend Books and Enola Stewart have long been familiar to serious mystery collectors. For years, Enola has put out the best annotated mystery book catalogues in the business. Until now they have been offset printed on 8½x11 paper from typed copy, secured with stables along one edge. Even in that format they have been invaluable. Though I have not bought more than a few items from Enola over the years (preferring, cheapskate that I am, to pick up my wants at garage sales and Salvation Army stores whenever possible), I have always enjoyed reading her catalogues, and I have saved them all for the extremely useful tools that they are. Now, however, Enola has outdone herself. Her latest catalogue, #25—64 pages, plus a cover—is typeset and printed on high quality, slick paper, and is simply the best damned catalogue in the world. If she has any copies left they are $5.00 each, and believe me they are worth every penny of it. In fact, as one who has had some experience with typesetting and printing costs, I honestly don't see how she keeps from losing money even at $5.00 a copy. The address is Gravesend Books, Box 235, Pocono Pines, PA 18350. If you don't already have a copy, get one now.

Time and space enough to mention some of the many paperback that have crossed my desk recently. Harper & Row, in its Perennial Library series, has reissued the following oldies but goodies, all at $1.95: Edmund Crispin, *Buried for Pleasure*; Francis Iles, *Malice Aforethought1* Cyril Hare, *Untimely Death*; Julian Symons, *Bogue's Fortune* and *The Broken Penny*. Charter also has a bunch of new releases: Dave Klein, *Blind Side*, $2.75; Robin Moore and Hugh McDonald, *The Black Sea Caper*, $2.50; John Creasey, *Salute the Toff*, $1.95; John Dickson Carr, *He Who Whispers*, $1.95; Art Bourgeau, *A Lonely Way to Die*, $1.95; Stuart Kaminsky, *You Bet Your Life*, $2.25; Kin Platt, *The Princess Stakes Murder*, $2.25; Nick Carter, *Eight Card Stud*, $2.25. Pocket Books has reissued Dick Francis's *Slayride* at $2.25, as well as Andrew Coburn's *The Trespassers* ($2.50) and Vincent Patrick's *The Pope of Greenwich Village* ($2.75). Pinnacle Books now has two books in its new Bennet series by Elliot Lewis in print: *Two Heads Are Better* and *Dirty Linen*, both $1.75. Lastly, Playboy Press has just published Phillips Lore's latest Leo Roi case, *The Looking Glass Murders*, and Michael Collins' latest Dan Fortune case, *The Brass Rainbow*, both $1.95.

# *The Nero Wolfe Saga*
## Part XIX
### By Guy M. Townsend

**Death of a Dude** (August 1968), published in 1969.

THE STORY ::: In the last week of the month's vacation Archie spends at Lily's Bar JR Ranch in Montana, a dude named Philip Brodell is shot to death at a nearby ranch, and Harvey Greve, who we encountered in "The Rodeo Murder" and who has been running Lily's ranch for the last four years, is arrested for the murder. Greve's suppositional motive: Brodell had, the previous summer, gotten Greve's daughter Alma pregnant and had not married her. To quote from a letter Archie writes to Wolfe on 2 August,

> Miss Rowan and I have decided Harvey didn't do it, and I'm stuck. If it had been plain and simple that he did it I would have been back there to keep your desk dusted when I was supposed to, day before yesterday.... (**But**) one will get you fifty that Harvey's clean. So you see how it is. I've got a job. Even if I had no obligation to Miss Rowan as her guest and an old friend, I've known Harvey Greve too long and too well to bow out and leave him in a squeeze.
> Of course from July 31, day before yesterday, I'm on leave of absence without pay. I hope to be back soon, but as it stands now I have no suggestions for a replacement for Harvey in the jug.... If you want to have Saul or Orrie at my desk, my strictly personal things are up in my room, so all my secrets are safe.... Give Theodore my regards and tell Fritz my first thought every morning is him—the breakfast in his kitchen I'm missing.

Actually, the mystery qua mystery is not particularly remarkable. The only way to get Harvey out is to get someone else in, and in the end that is what happens—through, it might be remarked, some very elementary detective work. What makes **Death of a Dude** noteworthy—and it is one of the most unusual episodes in the entire Saga—is the fact that the murder draws Wolfe completely out of his element. Attend...

WOLFE ::: In the late afternoon, a few days after Archie has mailed the above letter, a rickety old cab pulls up outside Lily's cabin: "The rear door of the taxi opened and a man climbed out, backwards. His big broad behind was Nero Wolfe's, and when he straightened up and turned around, so was his big broad front. Lily, at my elbow, said 'The mountain comes to Mohammed,' and we crossed the terrace to meet him." As Archie says, "Actually I am not absolutely essential to his convenience and comfort and welfare, nobody is, but he comes close to thinking I am," and rather than leave Archie in Montana indefinitely, Wolfe has made the collossal (for him) concession of coming west to hasten Harvey's release. Here's more on his arrival:

> Wolfe never shakes hands with a woman, and rarely with a man, but out in God's country people loosen up more, and when his hand left mine he actually offered it to Lily as he said, "My apologies. I should have telephoned. You probably resent unexpected callers, as I do, but I dislike the telephone and I have used it too much these two days. I'll not disturb you. I have to see Mr. Goodwin."
> "I make allowances," Lily said, "for callers who have come two thousand miles. Your luggage is in the car?"
> "It is in Timberburg. Near there. At a place called Shafer Creek Motel." To me: "I have a suggestion. That man is foolhardy and his vehicle may collapse at any moment. If one is available here, I'll send him off and you can drive me back after we have conferred."
> I turned to Lily. "As you know, he thinks all machinery acts on whims. If you won't need the car——"
> "This is silly," she said. To Wolfe: "Of course you'll sleep here. There's a room with a bed. After a day in airplanes and cars, you must be about to collapse. Archie will tell the man to go and bring your luggage, and I'll show you to your room. It has a bath. Have you had dinner?"
> "Miss Rowan. I will not impose——"
> "Now listen. You're used to having people at your mercy; now you're at mine. My car will not be available. Have you had dinner?"
> "I have eaten, yes. There will be a bill to pay at that place."
> I said I'd see to it and went and talked with the hackie.... When he had turned around and rolled down the lane I entered the cabin by the door to the long hall, kept going, found

the last door standing open, and entered. Wolfe was sitting in a chair by the open window with his chin down and his eyes closed.... He was probably, at that moment, the only man in Monroe County wearing a vest, which of course was the same dark blue as the jacket and trousers. He had changed at the motel; the cuffs and collar of the yellow shirt were smooth and clean. The blue four-in-hand was a little darker than the suit, and so was the homburg there on the table.

The cabbie returns with "a big tan leather suitcase which hadn't been out of the basement storeroom in the brownstone on West 35th Street for six years."

I helped him unpack. I admit that smacked of pampering, but I was curious. And as I had suspected when I had helped the hackie with the luggage, he had prepared for an extended stay when he left home; there was another suit—the brown worsted with little green specks—another pair of shoes, five shirts, ten pairs of socks, and so forth, including four books, one of which he may have brought along for possible reference. It was **Man's Rise to Civilization as Shown by the Indians of North America from Primeval Times to the Coming of the Industrial State**. By Peter Farb.

After Wolfe gets settled in with a bottle of Mountain Brewer, Butte, beer ("he held the glass until the bead was down just right, took a sip, made a face, took a healthy swig, and licked foam from his lips"), Archie speaks to him thusly:

"I'll give you just the skeleton," I said, "and the flesh and skin can be added as required. If I'm more outspoken than usual it's probably because I'm on leave of absence without pay. First, I do not think you came to haul me back. You know me almost as well as I know you. I wrote you that one will get you fifty that Harvey's clean, and you know I don't give those odds unless I'm dead sure. I think you came to get my facts and then hurry it up by telling me what to do."

Wolfe tries to reject Archie's basis for deciding Harvey's innocence, but Archie is ready for him:

The wrinkles of the frown were deeper. "This must be flummery. Certainly it isn't candor. Basing a firm conclusion of a man's guilt or innocence—not merely a conjecture—solely on your knowledge of his character? That's tommyrot and you know it. Pfui."

I gave him a wide grin. "Good. Now I've got you cold. You right, your brain isn't functioning properly. Less than three years ago you formed a firm conclusion on Orrie Cather's guilt or innocence solely on Saul Panzer's knowledge of his character. You also consulted Fred and me, but we were on the fence. Saul decided it. It's too bad I don't rate as high as Saul. And I have backing. Miss Rowan's conclusion is as firm as mine, but I admit she's a woman. There's a plane that leaves Helena at eleven in the morning. If I find I can't make it back in time to vote on November fifth I'll send for an absentee ballot."

Wolfe has to modify his style somewhat, since Archie is on leave of absence: "Bring Miss Rowan and—— No, you're on leave. Will you please ask Miss Rowan if it will be convenient for her to join us?" That doesn't last long, though, and Wolfe puts Archie back on salary again, retroactive to July 31, so that he can tell him not to do something that Archie wants to do (question a witness). Wolfe says, "I don't like to talk up to people, or down. I prefer eyes at a level." When Archie tells Wolfe he'll be expected to shake hands with folks while he is out in Montana, Wolfe says, "I resent any formality requiring bodily contact." But Archie says, "I concede that when he does shake he does it right." Unavoidably, Wolfe has to ride in more automobiles than usual this time out, and on one occasion he arrives in a car driven by someone other than Archie, and "he was in the front, which was unusual. In his Heron sedan, which I drive, he always sits in the back, where there is a strap for him to grab when the car decides to try climbing a curb or jostling some other car it doesn't like." When a man asks Wolfe if he plays Scrabble, "Wolfe shook his head. 'I don't play games. I like using words, not playing with them.'" Archie says to Wolfe, "You once said that a signal function of memory is discarding what we want to forget", and Lily tells him, "Archie has quoted you as saying that a guest is a jewel on the cushion of hospitality." Wolfe uses the word "plerophory", and at another place he remarks, "Man's brain, enlarged fortuitously, invented words in an ambitious effort to learn how to think, only to have them usurped by his emotions." When, in answer to Wolfe's question as to what one man wanted to do, another man answers "Nothing", Wolfe replies, "Nonsense. Only a saint wants to do nothing", and when the man asks Wolfe who said that, Wolfe says, "I seldom let another man speak for me, and when I do I name him." In an exchange with a woman Wolfe is told, "You know how a woman's mind works", to which he replies, "I do not. No one does." Archie says, "He made a face, as always when he had to use the phone", and in another place he remarks, "A corner of Wolfe's mouth raised a little—with him, a smile." Of Wolfe's aversion to going out of doors, Archie says "Many a time I had known him to postpone sending me on an errand if the weather was bad, and it took something very special, like a chance to get a specimen of a new orchid, to get him out of the house in rain or snow." At one point in this episode a woman enters a room and all the men stand except Wolfe: "Wolfe did not. He almost never does when a woman enters his office, and he had broken so many rules in the past three days that it must have given him real satisfaction to be able to stick to one." Wolfe says to a man he is questioning, "I once asked a woman ten thousand questions." Here is Wolfe in a highly unusual situation: "There he was, perched on a boulder surrounded by water dancing along, his pants rolled up above his knees, his feet in the water, and the sleeves of his yellow shirt rolled up." Of course, he has had to take his cufflinks out, and Archie tells us about them: "These two Muso emeralds, bigger than robin eggs, had once been in the earrings of a female who had died and left them to Wolfe in her will. Only a year ago a man had offered him thirty-five grand for them." The book Wolfe has brought along on his outing is Solzhenitsyn's **First Circle**.

ARCHIE::: When Archie settles down to investigate the case he purchases "a maginifying glass and a notebook that would go in my hip pocket.... On a job in New York I never go on an errand without those two articles." I don't believe there has ever been mention made of Archie carrying a magnifying glass around with him, though such glasses in the office have been mentioned at least once. Archie says "my favorite spot on earth is only a seven-minute walk from where I live, Nero Wolfe's house on West 35th Street: Herald Square, where you can see more different kinds of people in ten minutes than anywhere else I know of." He also tells us "I have never met a nineteen-year old boy who gave me the impression that he knew things I wouldn't understand, but three girls around that age have, and little Alma Greve was one of them." In a shop in Montana, "I went back to the paperbacks, picked one entitled **The Greek Way**, by Edith Hamilton, which I had heard mentioned by both Lily and Nero Wolfe, and went to a bench with it." Archie tells Wolfe "I named my horse, mine when I'm here, Pfui, because he's a little tricky." And he mentions this familiar item: "I raised one brow, which I often find helpful because he can't do it." When Wolfe decides that Archie is no longer on leave, we get an idea of exactly what Archie makes. Wolfe tells him to write himself a check for a week-and-a-half's pay, and Archie tells us, "I figured it on a sheet from my notebook—$600 minus federal income tax withheld $153.75, state income tax $33.00, and Social Security tax $23.88," leaving $389.37.

OTHER REGULARS ::: Lily, of course, has a starring role in this one. "On a list of the differences between Lily and me it would be near the top that I park so I won't have to back out when I leave and she doesn't." Archie speaks of some of her mannerisms: "If they had known Lily as well as I did they would have known that the little circular movement of the toe of her shoe meant that she was good and sore. Also one of her eyes, the left, was slightly narrower than the other, which was even worse." In another place he says, "On the way down the hall she asked no questions, which was like her and therefore no surprise. She knew from experience that if I knew something she should know, I had a tongue." At one point Lily says to Wolfe, "I have dined at your house." Archie says "A house guest at Lily's cabin might be anyone from a tired-out social worker to a famous composer of the kind of music I can get along without. That year there were three, counting me, which was par." One of these is a writer named Wade Worthy:

> He was ... a special kind of guest. He was doing a job. For two years Lily had collected material about her father, and when there was about half a ton of it she had started looking for someone to write the book, thinking that with the help of a friend of hers who was an editor at Parthenon Press it might take a week. It had taken nearly three months.... Lily's offer of a fat advance, with only half to be deducted from royalties—which the

editor strongly disapproved—had appealed to him (Worthy), and there he was at the typewriter, working on the outline. The title was to be A Stripe of the Tiger: The Life and Work of James Gilmore Rowan.

Archie mentions that Lily's dad had been "a Tammany Hall man who had made a pile building sewers and laying pavements." Finally, she calls Archie "Escamillo". With Lily is her maid Mimi, whose last name we learn is Diffand. Archie speaks of "Mimi's round blue eyes, which fitted her round face, which fitted all her other roundness.... We talked as freely in her presence as Wolfe and I did in Fritz's." Of the other regulars, only Saul receives any real mention. Wolfe puts him to work checking out some New York angles and later sends him to St. Louis. Archie mentions that it would cost Lily $500 a week to hire Saul who, he says elsewhere, "is better at almost anything than anyone else I know." Orrie Cather is barely mentioned, as being put in charge of the New York end when Saul goes to St. Louis.

ROUTINE AT THE BROWNSTONE ::: "Nearly all of my written communications to Nero Wolfe over the years have been on a sheet of memo pad, for Fritz to take up to his room on his breakfast tray, or put by me on his desk when he was upstairs in bed and I had returned from an evening errand. They has all begun 'NW' and ended 'AG' so this did too." Archie also mentions that "we never talked business during a meal."

ODDS & ENDS ::: Archie says that he and Lily have been to Blue Grouse Ridge often; "sometimes for berries and sometimes for young blue grouse which, about ten weeks old and grubbed almost exclusively on berries, were as good eating as anything Fritz had ever served. Of course it was against the law to take them, so of course we didn't overdo it."

**Please Pass the Guilt** (June 1969), published in 1973.

THE STORY ::: Doc Vollmer comes to the brownstone to ask Wolfe a favor. A psychaitrist friend of his runs a crisis clinic to which a man has been coming regularly complaining of blood on his hands which no one else can see. The man won't give his right name but agrees to talk to Wolfe is Wolfe will see him. He had, in fact, spoken to Archie on the phone and offered to pay Wolfe $100 an hour to ask him questions, but had been turned down. At Vollmer's request, Wolfe agrees to see the person the following evening at 9:00, and when he arrives Wolfe has Archie surreptitiously photograph him and then advise him of that fact, saying that there is no way they can help him without knowing who he is. The man then walks out with nothing being settled, though he does give them his card as he leaves. That might have been the end of that but for the fact that the bank account was perilously low and Archie recognizes the man's name as being that of one of the principals involved in the spectacular murder of Peter J. Odell, a vice president of the Continental Air Network, who had recently been blown to pieces by a bomb planted in another man's desk and set to go off when a certain drawer was opened. Archie decides on his own to go out and beat the bushes for a paying client, and eventually he lands the victim's widow as a client to the tune of $100,000. Archie engineers things so that Wolfe stays on the case, but it's a near thing. The detection is weaker than usual in this tale—which is made topical by references to the New York Mets, the Women's Liberation Movement, and Arab terrorists—but it's an entertaining episode as always, down to and including the closing melodramatic scene (which almost disguises the fact that the case is solved not so much by Wolfe's strength as by the villain's weakness).

WOLFE ::: Here is an obvious Sherlockian parallel: when Wolfe surprises Doc Vollmer by knowing about crisis intervention the following conversation ensues:

> Vollmer shook his head. "You know," he said, "you are the most improbable combination of ignorance and knowledge on earth. You don't know what a linebacker does. You don't know what a fugue is."
> "I try to know what I need to know. I make sure to know what I want to know."
> "What if it's unknowable?"
> "Only philosophers and fools waste time on the unknowable. I am neither."

Speaking of Doc Vollmer:

> He scowled. "I have told you a dozen times that 'Doc' is an obnoxious vulgarism.'
> "I keep forgetting."
> "Pfui. You never forget anything. It was deliberate."

This one is similar, though perhaps it would fit better in Archie's section: Wolfe says to Archie, "I complain of your conduct only directly, never by innuendo. You offend only deliberately, never by shortcoming." When the client, after paying a sizeable retainer to Wolfe to find out who killed her husband, tells him she knows who planted the bomb, Wolfe's reaction draws this comment from Archie: "I suppose Wolfe has been surprised by things people have said as often as you or me, but his ego has arranged with him not to show it and he rarely does. But that got him. His eyes stretched wide, as wide as I have ever seen them, then they narrowed at her, half closed, and he cleared his throat." Elsewhere, "Wolfe closed his eyes, and the forefinger of his right hand started making little circles on his desk blotter. But he wasn't tackling a tough one; his lips didn't move." Here's a new one regarding Wolfe's eyes:

> Since he was facing Abbott, he was in profile to me, but I had enough of his right eye to see what I call his slow-motion take. The eye closed, but so slow I couldn't see the motion of the lid. At least twenty seconds. He certainly wasn't giving Abbott a long wink, so the other eye was collaborating. They stayed shut about another twenty seconds, then opened in one, and he spoke.

At one point, at 10:05 in the evening, Wolfe "reached for his current book, **Grant Takes Command**, by Bruce Catton." In another place Archie tells us "Wolfe was at his desk with a book of stories by Turgenev, and that was bad too. When he's low he always picks something that he has already read more than once." This next exchange between Archie and Wolfe also reveals something of Wolfe's literary tastes: ARCHIE: "I don't claim the wording is perfect. I am not Norman Mailer." WOLFE: "Bah. That peacock? That blowhard?" ARCHIE: "All right, make it Hemingway." Among the uncommon words Wolfe uses this time out are amphigoric, subreption, and concupiscence. When a man says to Wolfe, "You use words, don't you?" Wolfe replies, "Yes. On occasion in six languages, which is a mere smattering. I would like to be able to communicate with any man alive." Regarding foreign languages, Wolfe says "Arabic is not one of my languages", but he appears to have understood a bit of it spoken by someone else. Wolfe, speaking of Archie, tells another person, "he once said that I ride words bareback." And there's this familiar item: "Wolfe's lips were tight. In his house, 'contact' is not a verb and never will be, and he means it." And here's one last word-related item: "'When I entered the office at 6:22, he was at his desk working on the Double-Crostic in the **Times**, and of course I didn't interrupt." And he's not just good at using words: Archie tells us "he is the best listener I know." Archie says, "he hates the phone"; "he leaves his house only for personal errands no one else can do, never on business"; "a corner of Wolfe's mouth was up a thirty-second of an inch. For him a broad grin"; "you wouldn't believe how easy and smooth he can remove his seventh of a ton off of a stool." When the client storms in and begins to berate Wolfe,

> Wolfe banged a fist on the desk and bellowed at her:
> "**Shut up!**"
> I don't know how he does it. His bellow is a loud explosion, a boom, as a bellow should be, but also it has an edge, it cuts, which doesn't seem possible.

Throughout this episode Wolfe has trouble maintaining his momentum:

> The fact was, Wolfe hadn't really bit into it. It was still just batting practice. He had taken the job and was committed, but there was still the slim chance that something might happen—the cops might get it or the client might quit—so he wouldn't have to sweat and slave. Also in my book there was the idea that I had once mentioned to him, the idea that it took a broil with Inspector Cramer to wind him up. Of course when I had offered it, he had fired me or I had quit, I forget which. But I hadn't dropped the idea.

And, as was mentioned earlier, Wolfe actually tries to quit on this one: on June 22, the case having started on the 3rd, Wolfe asks Archie how much expenses have been, and when Archie replies about $3,000 Wolfe says, "It will be a deduction on my tax return. Call Mrs. Odell and tell her I am quitting. Draw a check to her for the full amount of the retainer." Here is another, more subtle indication that things are not going well: a few minutes before noon Archie finds Wolfe "at his desk, with his oilstone and a can of oil on a sheet of paper, he was sharpening his penknife. Though he doesn't use it much, he sharpens it about once a week, but almost never at that time of day." Here's a new perspective on Wolfe's appearance: "When Wolfe faced Cramer in my chair with me in the red leather chair, I had his profile from the left instead of his right, and I had to adjust to it. I don't know why it made so much difference, but it did. His chin looked more pointed and his hair thicker." Archie has a little fun at Wolfe's expense when he tells him about an unorthodox meal he has eaten: "Of course I enjoyed my description of the picnic lunch in detail, but he didn't. He set his jaw and squinted at me, and did something he seldom does; he used profanity. 'Good God,' he growled. 'Are you—how do you feel?' " Just how particular Wolfe is about the orchids can be seen in Archie's remark that "Wolfe ... won't let even me cut his orchids." Wolfe says "I turn on the television rarely, only to confirm my opinion of it." Wolfe gets quite desperate in this one: a man arrives, "and when, in the office, he marched across and put out a hand, Wolfe took it. He seldom shakes hands with anybody, and never with strangers. He was low." Wolfe tells a man, "That's what makes us the unique animal, we want to know why and we try to find out. We even try to discover why we want to know why, though of course we never will." Up in the plant rooms Wolfe wears "his long-sleeved, yellow smock." He says, "I like eyes at a level." Lastly, he tells some people in the office that their conversation is not being recorded: "I give you that assurance on my word of honor, and those who know me would tell you that I would not tarnish that fine old pledge."

ARCHIE ::: Not much, this time. "When we haven't got a job or jobs going, I usually get out for a walk after breakfast, with or without an excuse like a trip to the bank." After one of the Thursday night sessions Archie says, "I will not report on the course of events at the poker table, except to say that having a complicated operation on my mind was no help to my wallet. I lost sixty-eight bucks." Archie doesn't like buttoned-down collars.

**WARNING: Information about one of the regular series characters is revealed in the OTHER REGULARS section of this episode. Knowing that information before reading the story will detract from the enjoyment of the story, so I suggest that anyone who has not yet read** Please Pass the Guilt **skip that section.**

OTHER REGULARS ::: Doc Vollmer, of course, appears at the beginning: "Vollmer crossed his long, lean legs and rubbed his narrow, lan jaw with a knuckle." Also at the beginning, when Archie is trying to line up a client without Wolfe's approval, he phones Lon Cohen on a Thursday evening and tells him to meet him at Rusterman's at 6:15. "The small room upstairs at Rusterman's had many memories for me, back to the days when Marko Vukcic was still alive and making it the best restaurant in New York, with frequent meals with his old friend Nero Wolfe helping to keep it the best. It was still better than good, as Lon Cohen remarked that evening." Several times, in fact. Archie says, "Just looking at Lon you would never guess, from his neat little face and his slick black hair, how sharp he is. But people who know him know, including the publisher of the Gazette, which is why he has a room to himself two doors down the hall from the publisher's room." Elsewhere Archie speaks of Lon's "eyes aimed about a foot above my head, as they often did when he was deciding whether to call or raise." Felix and Pierre are mentioned as doing the duties for Archie and Lon at the restaurant. Lily gets mentioned a lot, without actually appearing. At one point Archie has to break a baseball date with her: "I rang Lily Rowan and told her I was stuck for the day", but on another they do get to go to a game. On a Saturday night Archie goes "upstairs to dress properly for joining Lily Rowan's party at the Flamingo." This is on another Saturday: "I went and got my bag from the hall and let myself out, on my way to the garage for the Heron and then to the West Side Highway, headed for Lily Rowan's glade in Westchester. That's what she calls it, The Glade." The boys also get mentioned fairly often: "We had also decided to spend thirty-one dollars an hour, for as long as necessary, of the client's money, on Saul Panzer, Fred Durkin, and Orrie Cather—eight each for Fred and Orrie, and fifteen for Saul." Archie describes them thusly:

> Saul Panzer, who looks like a guy who was trying to sell encyclopedias but gave up and quit, and is actually the best operative alive; and big-footed, heavy-set Fred Durkin, who looks as if he wouldn't know what an encyclopedia is but actually bought a Britannica for his kids; and good-looking, six-foot Orrie Cather, who would trade an encyclopedia for a full-length mirror if he didn't already have one, but can handle a tough assignment when he needs to.

At one point Wolfe tells Fred, "Smile at people. Your smile is admirably deceptive." And of Orrie Archie says, "He can't quite ditch the idea that he should have my job. I admit that there is one little detail of detective work that he can do better than I can, but he doesn't know what it is so I won't name it." This case leads to some difficulties for both Fred and Orrie:

> Jill Cather, Orrie's wife, had threatened to walk out on him because he didn't get home until five in the morning Tuesday after taking the CAN female researcher to dinner and a show.... Fred Durkin, tailing a CAN male employee Thursday evening, had lost him, and he hates to lose a tale; and on Friday, Elaine, his oldest daughter, had admitted she was smoking grass.

Archie says of Saul, "he is as good as Wolfe at the trick of getting an answer to an unasked question." Saul behaves uncharacteristically in this next thing:

> That was a first—the first time Inspector Cramer had ever arrived and been escorted to the office in the middle of a session with the hired hands. And Saul Panzer did something he seldom does—he stunted. He was in the red leather chair, and when I ushered Cramer in I expected to find Saul on his feet, moving up another yellow chair to join Fred and Orrie, but no. He was staying put. Cramer, surprised, stood in the middle of the rug and said, loud, "Oh?" Wolfe, surprised at Saul, put his brows up. I, pretending I wasn't surprised, went to get a yellow chair. And damned if Cramer didn't cross in front of Fred and Orrie to my chair, swing it around, and park his fanny on it. As he sat, Saul, his lips a little tight to keep from grinning, got up and came to take the yellow chair I had brought. That left the red leather chair empty and I went and occupied it, sliding back and crossing my legs to show I was right at home.

Later, Cramer admits he is desperate and offers an exchange of information with Wolfe. He even agrees to have beer with Wolfe, but Wolfe, naturally, refuses what both men know is an impossible arrangement, and in the end Cramer departs in a huff as usual—"He put the glass, not empty, on the table, saw the cigar, and picked it up. I expected him to throw it at my wastebasket and miss as usual, but he stuck it in the beer glass, the chewed end down. He stood up." With Cramer present, Wolfe has this to say to Rowcliff: "You may know—or you may not—that there is an understanding between Mr. Cramer and me which he knows I observe. No conversation in this office with him present is recorded without his express consent. This is not being recorded." How did Rowcliff get into this? Ah, this is the episode in which Rowcliff gets his. It turns out that Rowcliff—J. M. Rowcliff this time—is married to the twin sister of one of the suspects, and that that suspect has gotten some inside information which Rowcliff lets slip. That's nothing too serious, really, but everyone is delighted to see him squirm. Saul is the first to come up with the connection: Saul tells Wolfe, "They have two children, a boy and a girl. Dennis (**the suspect**) and Diana (**Rowcliff's wife**) see each other quite often—as I said, twins." WOLFE: "Mr. Rowcliff and his wife?" SAUL: "Three people say they're happy. I know it's hard to believe that anybody could stand Rowcliff, but off duty he may be different." After hearing this Wolfe tells Saul, "More than satisfactory", and he tells Archie to put some champagne up to cool. Shortly afterward Fred arrives and tells Archie at the door, "If I hold it any longer I'll bust. Copes's twin sister is married to that sonofabitch Rowcliff." Archie says,

> Lieutenant Rowcliff has it in for all private detectives, but I admit he has a special reason for thinking the world would be better off without me. When he gets hot he stutters, and with me it must be catching, because when he's working on me and I see that he is getting close to that point, I start to stutter, especially on words that begin with g or t. It's a misdemeanor to interfere with a police officer in the performance of his duty, but how could he handle that?

Archie also says "It has been said that Rowcliff is handsome, and I'll concede that his six feet of meat is distributed well enough, but his face reminds me of a camel with a built-in sneer." Two more regulars, or rather, one more regular and one guy who we've met once before, need to be mentioned. Archie speaks of Theodore thusly: "Wolfe, still in the yellow smock, was at the sink washing his hands, and Theodore stood there with a paper towel ready for him. Theodore babies him, which is one of the reasons he is not my favorite human being." Finally, Archie gets some information from Avery Ballou at Federal Holding Corporation.

PHYSICAL ASPECTS ::: The car has already been mentioned. In another place Archie speaks of going "to the garage on Tenth Avenue where the Heron sedan that Wolfe owns and I drive is kept." Inside the brownstone, let's start with the basement. "In a corner of the big storage room there were two thick, old mattresses, no springs in them, which I had used a few times for targets to get bullets for comparison purposes.... The pool table (was) in the adjoining room, where it had been installed when Wolfe had decided he needed some violent exercise." Moving up a floor, the rack in the hallway is to the left of the front door as you face the door from the inside (on the right of someone entering the house from the front). In the office we are introduced to a new device, whose purpose is to take pictures of people without their knowing it:

> The only preparation needed took about six minutes—going to a cabinet for a fancy glass-and-metal jar with the sharpened ends of a dozen pencils protruding at the top, and placing it in a certain spot and a certain angle near the right edge of my desk, and putting a certain plug in a certain hidden outlet.

After the pictures have been taken, "I picked up the jar and told Ronald Seaver, 'Candid camera inside.' I removed a couple of pencils and held them up; they were only two-inch stubs. 'Leaving room for the camera below. It now has eight shots of you.' " Here's another new gadget, though the description of just where in or on Archie's desk it fits is not too clear: when Wolfe tells Archie to play a tape, "all I had to do was reach to the far corner of my desk to flip a switch. The playback, which was a honey and had cost $922.50, was on the desk at the back." Wolfe explains the other end of the system: "You should know, Miss Lugos, that this is being recorded electronically. The recorder is on a closet shelf in the kitchen, so that a man there can change the tape if necessary." Then there is "the big globe near the book shelves", which is also mentioned in this next quote: "Most of the people who enter that office for the first time have something eating them, but ever so often they notice one or more of the objects in view—the fourteen-by-twenty-six Keraghan rug or the three-foot globe or the floral display in the vase on Wolfe's desk." And here's an item we've seen a bit of lately: "I put paper in the typewriter and hit the keys. On the wall back of my desk is a mirror four feet high and six feet wide and in it I could see that Miss Haber was looking surprised. No female secretary thinks a man can use eight fingers and two thumbs on a typewriter." Archie says that he has a full face view of someone seated in the red leather chair, which establishes the orientation of the chair with relation to the chair at Archie's desk, and the following item is also useful in placing furniture in the office: when all the invited folks have been seated, "I went to Wolfe's desk and gave the kitchen button three stabs, and in a moment he came, detouring between the red leather chair and the wall to his desk, sat." Here's some new information about the contents of the office bookshelves: "on the third shelf from the bottom, at the left of the globe, were nine of them (that is, nine Bibles), four in different editions in English and five in foreign languages." And this is new, too: "the pictures on the wall—one of Socrates, one of Shakespeare, and an unwashed coal miner in oil by Sepesky. (According to Wolfe, man's three resources: intellect, imagination, and muscle.)" The safe is mentioned several times, and in it the cash box, whose supply is "always used bills". And here is something else new: "I went to the safe for the key to the locked cabinet where we keep various items that would be in the safe if there was room." Then there's "the alcove at the kitchen end" of the hall, and in it "the peephole that was covered on the office side by a trick picture of a waterfall." In the kitchen Archie "sat at the little table where I eat breakfast, reached for the house phone, and pushed the "P" button. After a two-minute wait, about par, the usual 'Yes?'" Also mentioned is the elevator which, Archie tells us, "will take up to 600 pounds." On the third floor Archie mentions "the color set, which, like everything else in my room, was bought and paid for by me." And finally, Archie gives us this arrangement for the plant rooms: "The three rooms—cool, medium, and warm—and opened the door of the potting room."

ROUTINE AT THE BROWNSTONE ::: Archie says that "the three employees of the Midtown Home Service Corporation who come once a week are always male because Wolfe insists on it." Two of them are named Andy and Sam, but in this instance they bring a woman named Lucile along, "a husky coal-black female with shoulders nearly as broad as mine", because it's getting to be tough to get men for the work. It is morning:

> Wolfe entered and told me good morning and went to put a cluster of acampe pachyglossa in the vase on his desk.
>
> He sat, got his nineteen stone (it looks better in stone than in pounds) arranged in his made-to-order chair, glanced at his desk calendar, and picked up the stack the mailman had brought.

The routine on the weekend differs. Apparently, Fritz can take off as he wishes, for on a Saturday Archie says "Fritz had left to spend a night and a day and another night as he saw fit, so before I went upstairs to dress properly for joining Lily Rowan's party at the Flamingo, I brought a bottle of beer." And Archie tells us "the Sunday household routine was different. Theodore didn't come on Sunday and Wolfe's morning with the orchids could be anything from twenty miinutes to four hours. Also Fritz might leave for the day right after breakfast or he might not." Archie adds, "for Sunday lunch with Fritz away he (**that is, Wolfe**) usually does something simple like eggs **au beurre noir** and a beet and watercress salad." Archie says "we keep both the **Times** and the **Gazette** for three weeks, sometimes longer." Dinner time at the brownstone is 7:15, so Archie doesn't dine at home on Thursday nights, since the regular poker game at Saul's apartment starts at 8:00, which would not give him time to finish. "When I'm not there Fritz usually answers the phone, but sometimes Wolfe does." Here's something new: "If I am in the office with company, and Wolfe isn't, when dinner's ready, Fritz comes and shuts the office door. That notifies me that food is ready to serve, and also it keeps the sound of voices from annoying Wolfe in the dining room across the hall, if I have to continue the conversation." Two more things from Archie: "I type all checks. That was the first one I had ever drawn for an even hundred grand"; "I have a sort of rule that when there is company and one of them is, or is supposed to be, a murderer, the place for him or her is the front row nearest me."

ODDS & ENDS ::: At the start of this case the financial situation is pretty grave:

> We needed a job. In the past five months, the first five of 1969, we had had only six cases, and the fee had gone to five figures in only one of them—getting a damn fool out of a nasty mess with a bunch of smoothies he should have been on to at the first contact. So the checking account balance had lost a lot of weight, and to meet the upkeep of the old brownstone, including the weekly payroll for Theodore and Fritz and me, by about the middle of July Wolfe would have to turn some documents into cash, and that should be prevented if possible.

Just how slim things are is revealed once the case begins and Archie reports that if they have to send the retainer back "the balance will be a little under six thousand dollars."

> I was at my desk in the office, scowling at the entries in a little looseleaf book which I call The Nero Wolfe Backlog. It contained a list of certain items that were in his safe deposit box at the Continental Trust Company, and I was considering which one or ones should be disposed of at the current market price if I was asked for a suggestion.

Archie needs a boat to take a witness out on so he borrows one from a former client: "The name of the boat was **Happygolucky**. I had borrowed it from a man named Sopko, who had once paid Wolfe $7,372.40, including expenses, for getting his son out of a deep hole he had stumbled into." Finally, "I got to Sam's diner on Tenth Avenue a little after one and emjoyed rye bread and baked beans, two items that never appear at Wolfe's table."

**WARNING: Do not read the next episode before you have read the book. Everything is revealed herein, and reading this will spoil a super book unless you've already read it.**

**A Family Affair** (October-November, 1974), published in 1975.

THE STORY ::: This is the last recorded episode of the Saga, and in many ways it is one of the best and most interesting. It is a "Monday night-Tuesday morning late in October" and Archie has just gotten home from a date with Lily when, at 1:10 a.m., the doorbell rings. It is Pierre Ducos, from Rusterman's, and he is very obviously frightened and wants to see Wolfe. He won't tell Archie what it's about except to say that someone is trying to kill him. Rather than wake Wolfe up at that hour, Archie puts Pierre in the South Room to spend the night, but before Archie can get undressed and in bed himself Pierre gets blown to pieces by a bomb disguised as a cigar tube. This is a bit of a facer for the boys in the brownstone. Here's a murder committed actually in Wolfe's house, and what's more the victim is a long-time acquaintance of both Wolfe and Archie. Furthermore, Archie himself could have been the dead man had he unscrewed the cap of the tube, so Wolfe takes the murder personally and determines to catch the murderer. And for no fee—it is, as he says, a family affair. The investigation soon turns up a connection with the recent murder of Harvey H. Bassett, an executive with National Electronics Industries who, it turns out, had an obsession about Watergate: "He made the equipment for electronic recording ... and he thought Nixon had debased it. Polluted it. He wanted to do something about it but didn't know what." This, as Archie points out, "put an entirely new face on it. Knowing Wolfe as I did, that was obvious." As we will see below, Wolfe has some very strong views on the subject of Watergate and Richard Nixon. Determined, as they both are, to be personally responsible for bringing down the murderer, Wolfe and Archie are even less cooperative with the police than usual, and this results in their licenses being suspended and, in time, their actually being locked up for a time as material witnesses. Parker springs them, though, and they continue with the investigation which eventually reveals that this is a family affair in more ways than one. To wit, the murderer, who strikes again before he is exposed, is Orrie Cather himself. When this finally comes out, Archie, Saul and Fred have a conference, leaving Wolfe out of it. Archie is talking to Saul and Fred:

> Two facts. One, Orrie has asked for it and has to get it. He has bought it, and it has to be delivered. Two, Nero Wolfe, the great detective, is hogtied. He can't make a move. If he goes by the book, collects the pieces and hands Cramer the package, he will have to get on the witness stand and answer questions under oath about a man he has used and trusted for years. He wouldn't do that, he would rather spend ten years behind bars than do that. You know damn well he wouldn't, and I'm glad he wouldn't. All of us would have to answer questions in public about a guy we have worked with and played pinochle with.... I don't think he (**Wolfe**) could stand the sight of Orrie Cather. That's why we had to meet here (in **Saul's apartment**) instead of at the office.

The three of them get Orrie up to Saul's place and explain the situation to him. Archie does most of the talking:

> I'll just tell you what we're going to do. We're going to make it impossible for you to live. I'm going to see Jill (**Orrie's wife**) tomorrow, or Saul is. You'r through with her. You're through with any kind of work, not only in New York. Anywhere in the world. You're through with any kind of contact with people that means anything. You know us and you know Nero Wolfe. We know what it will cost us, Nero Wolfe in money and us in time and effort, but that's what we have to pay for not realizing long ago that some day, some how, we would be sorry we didn't cross you off.

Orrie tells Archie that they can't prove anything, but Archie replies, "We don't have to prove it. We don't want to prove it. I told you, we're not going to turn you in, we're going to make it impossible for you to live. Actually, we **could** prove it, but you know what it would mean, especially for Nero Wolfe." Before this conversation takes place the boys have frisked Orrie and found the twin of the bomb that killed Pierre in his pocket. When they are through talking with him they give him the bomb back. The next morning Saul and Fred and Archie are in the office with Wolfe, and Saul tells Wolfe, "we decided to make him kill himself." When he hears this, "Wolfe says, 'Satisfactory,' but he said it only with his eyes. His mouth stayed shut tight." Moments later the doorbell rings, followed almost instantly by an explosion: Orrie has blown himself up on the front stoop of the brownstone. All in all, this is one of the very best episodes in the Saga, a splendid note for the series to end on.

WOLFE ::: When the explosion occurs in the South Room Archie, after first checking the door to that room and finding it bolted from the inside, rushes downstairs to check on Wolfe. (Archie doesn't mention turning the gong off, but it doesn't appear to sound when he goes to Wolfe's door.)

> I ran down one flight, saw that the door to Wolfe's room was intact, and went and knocked on it. My usual three, a little spaced. I really did, and his voice came.
> "Archie?"
> I opened the door and entered and flipped the light switch. I don't know why he looks bigger in those yellow pajamas than in clothes. Not fatter, just bigger. He had pushed back the yellow electric blanket and black sheet and was sitting up.

Archie goes up to the South Room via the fire escape. While he is looking the room over

> something hit the door three hard knocks, and I went and slid the bolt and opened it and there was Wolfe. He keeps one of his canes in the stand in the downstairs hall and the other four on a rack in his room, and he was gripping the biggest and toughest one with a knob the size of my fist, which he says is Montenegrin applewood.

After looking at the devastation done to Pierre and to the room, Wolfe says to Archie, "I am going to my room and bolt the door. I will stay there until they have come and gone and I will see no one. Tell Fritz that when he brings my breakfast he will make sure that no one is near. When Theodore comes, tell him not to expect me." And with that, "he went, still gripping the Montenegrin applewood by the small end. I didn't hear the elevator, so he took the stairs, which he rarely does. Barefoot." But it is not Wolfe's intent to hide from the problem; indeed, he bestirs himself to unparalleled activity (if we discount the **Black Mountain** episode). Receiving a no from Archie to the question "Do you know of any source of information about Pierre other than the restaurant?", Wolfe goes to Rusterman's and questions the help. He and Archie also have lunch there, after which he asks Archie.

> "Can you have the car brought to the side entrance?"
> "Now?"
> "Yes. We're going to see Pierre's father."
> I stared at him. "We?"
> "Yes. If you brought him to the office we would be interrupted. Since Mr. Crammer and the District Attorney have been unable to find us, there may already be a warrant."
> "I could bring him here."
> "At nearly eighty, he may not be able to walk. Also the daughter may be there."
> "Parking in the fifties is impossible. There may be three or four flights and no elevator."
> "We'll see. Can it be brought to the side entrance?"
> I said of cou se and got his coat and hat. It certainly was all in the family. For a client, no matter how urgent or how big a fee, it had never come to this and never would."

Not surprisingly, Cramer is not pleased with what the boys are doing and he comes to the brownstone and proceeds to berate Wolfe, but Wolfe cuts him short: " '**Shut up!**' Cramer gawked. He had heard Wolfe tell a hundred people to shut up, and I had heard him tell a thousand, including me, but never Cramer. He didn't believe it." Wolfe doesn't stop at that:

> Wolfe aimed a straight finger at him, up at his face, another first. "If I sound uncivil, I do not apologize. I am in a rage and out of control. Whether you have warrants or not, arrest us now and take us; let's get that over with. I have a job to do." He extended his arms, stretched out, the wrists together for handcuffs. Beautiful. I would have loved to do it too, but that would have been piling it on.

Wolfe acknowledges that he is out of control in more ways than one, as the next few quotes will show. Archie types up a report of the conversation in which he learns of the Nixon connection:

> Three pages. He read the last page twice, looked at me with his eyes half shut, and said, "By God."
> I stared at him. I may have gaped. He never says by god, and he said it with a capital G. So I didn't say anything.
> He did. "Was he gibbering? Was it flummery?"
> "No sir. It was straight."

Archie says, "He probably knew more about every angle of Watergate than any dozen of his fellow citizens, for instance the first names of Haldeman's grandparents." And when Archie hands him a list of the people who were present at the conversation when the Nixon connection came up, " 'I am not easily overwhelmed,' he said. 'If I could have them her now, all of them, I would pretermit dinner.' " When Saul and Fred and Orrie are first brought in, Wolfe explains about the Nixon problem:

> He (Archie) knew that for the first time in my life I had an itch that could not be relieved—that I hankered for something I couldn't get. He knew that I would have given all of my orchids—well, most of them—to have an effective hand in the disclosure of the malfeasance of Richard Nixon. I also dictated to him a letter offering my services to Mr. Jaworski, and he typed it, but it wasn't sent. I tore it up.... Well, Mr. Nixon is now out, no longer in command of our ship of state, no longer the voice of authority to us and of America to the world, but the record is by no means complete. History will dig at it for a century.... Now. You have always trusted my judgment and followed instructions without question. Now you can't. I don't. On this I can't be sure my intellect will ignore the goad of my emotions.

Wolfe comments, "Richard Nixon's main buoy in his frantic effort to keep himself afloat, was his plea of national security." Wolfe also tells another person, "I don't have an obsession, but I too am attentive to the skullduggery of Richard Nixon and his crew." This next item shows even more of Wolfe's remarkable activity in this episode:

> When we left the dining room (at 2:10, after lunch) he ... had announced that he was going to go and vote and reached to the rack for the coat he had brought down. Certainly, voting was one of the few personal errands that got him out in any weather. But at a quarter past six he hadn't come back and that was ridiculous. Four hours. All bets were off. He was in a hospital or in the morgue, or in an airplane headed for Montenegro. I was regretting that I hadn't turned on the six-o'clock news and considered whether to start phoning now or wait until after dinner when the doorbell rang and I went to the hall and there he was. He never carried keys. I went and opened the door and he entered, said, "I decided to do an errand,' and unbuttoned his coat.
> I said, "Much traffic?"
> He said, "Of course. There always is."

We learn later that Wolfe's errand was actually a trip to Saul's apartment, necessitated, in Wolfe's eyes, by what he thought Archie would do if he knew that Orrie was the killer. Saul tells Archie about it:

> "Archie, this is the first time I ever knew you to miss one completely. I supposed you had it figured and was enjoying it. You actually didn't know that he thought you'd kill him? That he thinks he knows you would?"
> The letter dropped from my hand, and I guess my mouth dropped open as I turned. "Balls," I said.
> "But he does. He says you wouldn't do it with a gun or a club, just with your hands. You'd hit him so hard you'd break his neck, or you'd throw him so hard and so far he'd break his neck when he landed. I didn't try to argue him out of it, because he knew it."
> "I thought he knew me. And you think it's funny."
> "I know it's funny. He does know you. I thought you knew him. It's just that he wants to kill him himself. So do I. So do you."

This next long one has a good bit of everything, so perhaps its length will be forgiven:

> Three days' mail was on his desk, and he went at it. First, as usual, a quick once-through, dropping about half in the wastebasket. Of course I had chucked most of the circulars and other junk. He answers nearly all real letters, especially handwritten ones, because, he once told me, it is a mandate of civility. Also, I said, all he had to do was talk to me and he loved to talk, and he nodded and said that when he had to write them by hand he hadn't answered any. I said then he wasn't civilized, and that started him off on one of his hair-splitting speeches. We answered about twenty letters, three or four from orchid collectors and buffs as usual, with a few interruptions, phone calls from Parker and Lon Cohen and Fred Durkin. When I swiveled to my desk I was surprised to see him go to the shelves for a book—Fitzgerald's translation of the Iliad. In the mail there had been an inscribed copy of Herblock's new book, Special Report, with about a thousand cartoons of Nixon, but apparently he no longer needed to read or look at pictures about it because he was working on it. So he sat and read about a phony horse instead of a phony statesman.

Archie says Wolfe "worked hard at comparing Fitzgerald's **Iliad** with the three other translations he brought over from the shelf. That was risky because they were on a high shelf and he had to use the stool." On the subject of Wolfe's books, Archie says to him, "I've been looking through that book you just bought, **The Southern Voyage**, by that admiral." Also, Wolfe says of Betty Friedan's **Feminine Mystique**, "I read about a third of it." Early in this episode Wolfe summons Archie to his bedroom; "He was seated at the table between the windows, with a book.... As I crossed to him he put the book down—**The Palace Guard** by Dan Rather and Gary Gales—and growled, 'Good morning.'" Wolfe tells Archie, "As you know, I prefer not to read when I may be interrupted at any moment." And speaking of interruptions, his routine in the plant rooms is repeatedly interrupted in this episode. On the day following the explosion he doesn't go up at all. He misses his afternoon session when he goes to vote and to see Saul. He misses both sessions while he is in jail, and he misses at least one other morning session. And one morning when a person comes to the brownstone at twelve minutes until eleven, Wolfe says, "I'll be down at once." Archie says, "When he wants to give something a good look and is in the office at his desk, in the one chair that he thoroughly approves, he leans back and shuts his eyes, but the back of that chair (**the one in his bedroom**) isn't the right angle for it, so he just squinted and pulled at his ear lobe. A full two minutes." This doesn't do much good, though:

> "Nothing," he said. "Nothing whatever."
> "Right. Because you're the greatest detective in the world. Stebbins doesn't believe it. He thinks he (**Pierre**) told me something, maybe not a name but something, and I left it out because we want to get him ourselves. Of course we do, at least I do. I might have unscrewed the cap of that tube myself, so I owe him something."
> "So do I. In my own house, asleep in my own bed, and that. That—that..."
> I raised my brows at him. That was a first. The first time in my long experience that he had ever been at a loss for words.

One of the people Wolfe interviews at Rusterman's is Philip Correla, who Wolfe remembers: "'You once disagreed with me about **Rouennaise** sauce.' 'Yes, sir. You said no bay leaf.' 'I nearly always say no bay leaf. Tradition should be respected but not sanctified.'" He says, "I prefer eyes at a level." Archie says, "He hates to tilt his head to look up at someone standing." Here is a new mannerism Archie has not mentioned before: "He got the tips of his vest between thumb and finger, both hands, and pulled down. He didn't know he did that, and I never mentioned it. It was a sign that his insides had decided that it was time to eat." And while we are on the subjects of eating and Rusterman's, "Whenever he eats at Rusterman's, Wolfe has a problem. There's a conflict. On the one hand, Fritz is the best cook in the world, and on the other hand, loyalty to the memory of Marko Vukcic won't admit that there is anything wrong with anything served in that restaurant." And there's the old familiar "business is never to be mentioned at the table." Archie says, of the trip to Pierre's apartment,

> When we were in and rolling, I suggested going to the garage and leaving the Heron, which Wolfe owns and I drive, and taking a taxi, but he thinks a moving vehicle with anyone but me at the wheel is even a bigger risk and vetoed it.

And, he adds, "He doesn't talk when he's walking or in the car." There's a bit about the women's liberation movement in this episode (as in the last), and when Archie calls a woman a "Women's Libber" Wolfe says, "You know I will not tolerate that locution", so Archie says, "All right, Liberationist." When Archie comes in a little after eleven at night he expects that "Wolfe would be deep in either a book or a crossword puzzle, but he wasn't. In one of my desk drawers I keep street maps of all five New York boroughs, and he had them, with Manhattan spread out covering his desk blotter and then some. To my knowledge it was the first time that he had ever given it a look." Archie says Philip and Felix are "greeted by Wolfe's most exaggerated nod, a full half-inch." Wolfe comes into the office and finds Archie has returned: "He went to his desk and sat and said, 'You're back.' He rarely says things that are obvious, but he says that fairly often because it's a miracle that I'm not limping or bleeding after spending hours out in the concrete jungle." After a conference in the office early in the case Archie, referring to Saul and Fred and Orrie, says that all "were on their feet, including Wolfe. He had shaken hands with them when they arrived, but they didn't offer now because they knew he didn't like it." In conversation with Wolfe a man quotes Thomas More, which Archie says was "Not a good start. Wolfe didn't like quoters, and he was down on More because he had smeared Richard III." When a man says to Wolfe, "You admit it?" the following transpires: "Wolfe wiggled a finger. That was regression—I looked it up. He had quit finger-wiggling a couple of years back. 'Don't do that,' he said. 'Calling a statement an admission is one of the oldest and scrubbiest lawyers' tricks, and you're not a lawyer. I state it.' " Still on words, Archie says "I have tried to talk him out of that 'whom.' Only highbrows and grandstanders and schoolteachers say 'whom,' and he knows it. It's the mule in him." Wolfe says, "There is only one object on earth that frightens me: a physicist working on a new trick." Archie says "He always moves as if he weighted a twelfth of a ton instead of a seventh." Archie comes in to the office and finds that "Wolfe was at his desk with the middle drawer open, counting beer-bottle caps." Wolfe also works a crossword puzzle in this one. After Wolfe's sojourn in jail a man tells him that he doesn't look like he has just spent time there; " 'I have spent more time in a dirtier jail,' Wolfe said. 'In Algiers.' " When Cramer has coffee at the borwnstone, "Wolfe poured, and he remembered that Cramer took sugar and cream, though it had been at least three years since he had had coffee with us." When the case is over, Wolfe explains it all to Cramer—putting it in the form of "a long and elaborate supposition", of course—and he tells Cramer what he is going to do with himself for a while: "Read books, drink beer, discuss food with Fritz, logomachize with Archie. Perhaps chat with you if you have occasion to drop in. I'm loose, Mr. Cramer. I'm at peace." Archie says "he can take coffee hotter than I can." Wolfe says that a thing under discussion "could be construed as a rejection of free will, and I do **not** reject it." Cramer, as usual, leaves in a huff, saying "I'm going home and try to get some sleep. You probably have never had to try to get some sleep. You probably never will.'" When he is gone Wolfe says to Archie, "Will you bring brandy, Archie? And two glasses. If Fritz is up, bring him and three glasses. We'll try to get some sleep." Finally, here are descriptions of a couple of Wolfe's suits. Fritz tells Archie that Wolfe has on "the dark brown with little stripes. Yellow shirt and brown tie." And when he is about to be taken to jail Wolfe goes up to his room to change, "But he had changed not to his oldest suit but his newest one—a soft light-brown with tiny yellow specks that you could see only under a strong light. He had paid Boynton $345.00 for it only a month ago. The same shirt, yellow of course, but another tie, solid dark-brown silk." Oops, missed this one—when the fellows are in the office having drinks, Archie thought "Wolfe would ring for beer, but he didn't, and that was a bad sign. When he skips beer, have your raincoat and rubbers handy."

ARCHIE ::: When Archie was preparing for bed, after settling Pierre down in the South Room, he was thinking "I wouldn't get my eight hours. When I get in that late I usually set my radio-alarm at nine-thirty." Of course he is delayed in getting to bed that night, but when he finally makes it "I was asleep two minutes after I got flat, and I stayed asleep. I don't brag about my sleeping because I suspect it shows that I'm primitive or vulgar or something, but I admit it." And when he gets up the next day this remarkable thing takes place: "As I was buttering the third slice of toast the phone rang. I counted. It rang twelve times and stopped. In a couple of minutes Fritz said, 'I never saw you do that before.' " Archie's egalitarian instincts emerge in this one: "Fritz came in with the tray. There's something I don't like about my taking something from a tray held by Fritz, and as he reached Wolfe's desk I went and got my gin and tonic." I don't think we've encountered this one before: "I went to the hall and to the rack for my coat. No hat. The thermometer outside said 38, more like December than October, no sun, but I have rules too. No hat before Thanksgiving.

Rain or snow is good for hair." Archie says, "One of my more useless habits is timing all walks, though it may be helpful only about one time in a hundred." He mentions again that "I had been born in Ohio." In Rusterman's, "I went to the bar and ordered an Irish with water on the side." Of his job, Archie says "I am supposed to badger him. That's one of the forty-four things I get paid for." And here's a long and interesting one:

> I admit that, like everybody else, I like to think that I have hunches. For instance, the time that I was in the office of the head of a Wall Street brokerage firm and he brought in four members of his staff, and after talking with them five minutes I thought I knew which one of them had been selling information to another firm, and two weeks later he confessed. Or the time a woman came and asked Wolfe to find out who had taken her emerald and ruby bracelets, and when she left I had told him she had given them to her nephew, and he had taken it on anyhow because he wanted to buy some orchid plants, and had regretted it later when he had to sue to get his fee. By the way, that was one of the reasons he thought I could size up any woman in ten minutes.

Regarding Archie's relationship with Lily, about which there is a good bit in the next section, Archie says, "When I am dressing and getting packed for a weekend at Lily Rowan's pad in Westchester, which she calls The Glade, I thoroughly approve of the outlook." This time, however, the trip gets cancelled by another murder, and Archie goes up to the plant rooms to tell Wolfe: "That was the third time, or maybe the fourth, I went down the aisles without seeing a thing. The benches could have been empty." Archie says "Of the lock-ups I have slept in, including White Plains, only thirty miles, New York is the worst. The worst for everything—food, dirt, smell, companionship, pieces of everything from newspapers to another blanket—everything." He and Wolfe, incidentally, are locked up for 51 house. Here's Archie on voting.

> The most interesting incident Tuesday morning was my walking to a building on Thhirty-fourth Street to enter a booth and push levers on a voting machine. I have never understood why anybody passes up that bargain. It doesn't cost a cent, and for that couple of minutes you're the star of the show, with top billing. It's the only way that really counts for you to say I'm it, I'm the one that decides what's going to happen and who's going to make it happen. It's the only time I feel important and know I have a right to. Wonderful. Sometimes the feeling lasts all the way home if somebody doesn't bump me.

In case you are wondering, Archie says "I had split the ticket.... I had voted for Carey but not for Clark." Archie says, "I use the elevator about once a month, and never alone." Finally, in the huddle with Saul and Fred before tackling Orrie, Archie says that everyone knew before he did. " 'You had a hurdle we didn't have,' Saul said. 'You knew Orrie wanted your job and thought he might get it. You've always gone easy on him, made allowances for him that Fred or I wouldn't make. It's in your reports. You had blinders that we didn't.' "

OTHER REGULARS ::: Let's start with Lily, about whose relationship with Archie we learn a great deal this time. Archie says he has "met only about a tenth of the characters—poets from Bolivia, pianists from Hungary, girls from Wyoming or Utah—who had been given a hand by Lily Rowan." Archie phones her: "After eight rings, par for that number, a voice came. 'Hello?' She always makes it a question." After they talk, "We hung up. That's one of the many good points: we hung up." Archie says "I ... like the manners" at Lily's place. "Lily nearly always opens the door herself, and she doesn't lift a hand when a man takes his coat off in the vestibule. We usually don't kiss for a greeting, but that time she put her hands on my arms and offered, and I accepted. More, I returned thecompliment." In this conversation Archie speaks first, then Lily:

> "I want to make it perfectly clear that——"
> "Don't do that! I've told you. Even a joke about him turns my stomach."
> "You're too careless with your pronouns. Your hims. Your first him's opinion of your second him is about the same as yours. So is mine."

The first him, of course, is Wolfe, and the second is Nixon. Lily says, "My god, Escamillo, is it possible that I am capable of jealousy? Of course, if I could be about anybody, it would be about you." Archie asks Lily to help him out by getting some information from one of her acquaintances: "She took a bite of celery and chewed. That's another good point: her face is just as attractive when she is chewing celery or even a good big bit of steak. She swallowed. 'This is the third time you've asked me to help,' she said. 'I didn't mind the other two. In fact I enjoyed it.' " Later Archie remarks, "But she didn't ask what or how or why or when, although she knew we were working on it. Incredible. I'd buy a pedestal and put her on it if I thought she would stay. She would either fall off or climb down, I don't know which." Finally, this happens at Lily's place: "I put down my glass, bent down to take her slipper off—blue silk or something with streaks of gold or something—poured a couple of ounces of champagne in it, lifted it to my mouth and drank." Mimi is around, and her cooking ability gets commented on. Lily says, "Mimi will do a quick omelet. Even he (**meaning Wolfe**) admitted she could do an omelet. At the ranch." Also, Archie says "Mimi is good at puddings and parfaits and pastries. Also at coffee." Understandably, there is a good bit about the boys in this one:

> I forget who once called them the Three Musketeers. Saul was in the red leather chair, and Fred and Orrie were in the two yellow ones I had moved up to face Wolfe's desk. Saul had brandy, Orrie had vodka and tonic, Fred had bourbon, I had milk, and Wolfe had beer.
>
> Saul Panzer was two inches shorter, much less presentable with his big ears and unpressed pants, and in some ways smarter than me. Fred Durkin was one inch shorter, two inches broader, heavier-bearded, and in some ways a little more gullible. Orrie Cather was half an inch taller, a lot handsomer, and a little vainer. He was still sure he should have my job and thought it was conceivable that someday he would. He also thought he was twice as attractive to all women under forty, and I guess he was. He could say let's look at the record.

Wolfe tells a man, "I'm paying three men forty dollars an hour to inquire about you." On another occasion the boys are in the office, and "for a change we all had martinis. Fred didn't like the taste of gin but he wanted to be sociable." Fred says, "I've got two families. I don't live here like Archie, but I like to think this is my **professional** family." Fred actually knew Orrie was guilty before anyone else, but he thought he must be wrong because Wolfe hadn't figured it out yet. By the way, Saul and Fred and Orrie are also arrested when Wolfe and Archie are, and are sprung a day after they are by Parker. Archie makes this comment about Saul: "He laughed. Not with his mouth, no noise; he laughed with his eyes, and by shaking his head." (This is when Saul discovers that Archie doesn't know that Wolfe thinks Archie will kill Orrie when he finds out the truth.) Archie and Saul travel to Saul's place in Saul's car:

> We left the car in the garage on Thirty-ninth Street where he keeps it and walked a couple of blocks. He lives alone on the top floor of a remodeled house on Thirty-eighth Street between Lexington and Third. The living room is big, lighted with two floor lamps and two table lamps. One wall had windows, one was solid with books, and the other two had doors to the closet and hall, and pictures, and shelves that were cluttered with everything from chunks of minerals to walrus tusks. In the far corner was a grand piano. The telephone was on a desk between windows. He was the only operative in New York who asked and got twenty dollarws an hour that year, and he had uses for it.
>
> When I sat at the desk and started to dial, he left for the bedroom, where there's an extension.

At one point Saul says of Orrie, "He often does jobs for Del Bascom." The night following the confrontation of Orrie with his guilt, Archie "slept on the couch in Saul's living room." Archie tells us that "Saul grows chives in a sixteen-inch box in his kitchen window." And: "Saul, always a good host, had a couple of chairs in place in front of the couch and liquids on the coffee table—Ten Mile bourbon for Fred and me and brandy for him." And then Orrie. 'As I think I mentioned, Orrie was half an inch taller than me and fully as broad, without a flabby ounce on him." In his vanity, Orrie is consistent to the end: after he blows himself up on the brownstone steps, Archie says "There was nothing much wrong with his face. He had liked his face too much to hold it the way Pierre had held it." We don't really larn a great deal about Pierre. Archie says, "Pierre had often fed me. He had fed many people, in one of the three rooms upstairs at Rusterman's restaurant. I had never seen him anywhere else.... I knew his age, fifty-two." A friend of his at the restaurant says, "He was a fine man, an honest man. He wasn't perfect, he had that one fault, he bet too much on horse races, but he knew he did and he tried to stop." And Lily says of him, "As you know, I think he was the best waiter that ever fed me. He remembered that I like my fork at the right of my plate after just one time." There are, of course, other regulars associated with Rusterman's:

> The top floor at Rusterman's restaurant was once the living quarters of Marko Vukcic, its owner, who had been Wolfe's boyhood friend in Montenegro and one of the only three men I knew who called him by his first name. For a year or so after Marko's death it had been unoccupied, and then Felix, who had been left a one-third share and ran the restaurant under Wolfe's supervision as trustee, had moved in with his wife and two children. Soon the children had got married and left.
>
> At twenty-five minutes to one, Wolfe and I were seated at a table near a window on that floor which looked down on Madison Avenue. Felix, slim and trim, elegant in blue-black and white for the lunch customers....

Archie later tells a man that "for a couple of years Nero Wolfe was in charge of Rusterman's restaurant as trustee, and a man named Felix Mauer was under him. Now Felix is in charge, but he often asks Nero Wolfe for advice, and Mr. Wolfe and I often eat there." Rusterman's, which we learn is closed on Sundays, has a large staff: "Of the seventy-some at Rusterman's altogether, there were few that Wolfe had never seen, only seven or eight who had come since he had bowed out as trustee." Archie talks on the phone several times to Lon Cohen, and goes to his office: "It took nine minutes to the Gazette building. Lon Cohen's room, two doors down the hall from the publisher's on the twentieth floor, barely had enough space for a big desk with three phones on it, one chair besides his, and shelves with a few books and a thousand newspapers." On one occasion he gets a call "from Lon Cohen to say that they had been sorry not to get my usual contribution at the poker game—which was libel, since I win as often as he does and nearly as often as Saul Panzer." And when Orrie goes to pieces, so to speak, in front of the brownstone, Archie says to Saul and Fred, "Stand by. I'm going in and ring Lon Cohen. I owe him something." And then there's good old Fritz, who's always around. After the explosion in the South Room, Archie goes down to the basement "to knock on Fritz's door and call my name, loud. He's a sound sleeper, but in half a minute the door opened. The tail of his white nightshirt flapped in the breeze from the open window. Our pajamas-versus-nightshirt debate will never be settled." Archie says, "Fritz entered (the office). To announce a meal he always comes in three steps, never four." Tom, at the garage where the Heron is kept, is mentioned (for the first and only time?), and Archie mentions another occasional regular in this complaint to Wolfe about the postal service: "The letter from Hewitt about a new orchid was mailed last Saturday. Six days from Long Island to Manhattan. Forty-two miles. I could walk it in one day." And Theodore: "I concede that as an orchid man Theodore may be as good as he thinks he is, but as a boon companion—a term I once looked up because Wolfe told me it was trite and shouldn't be used—you can have him." Parker, of course, is there to spring Wolfe, Archie and the boys, and at another time Archie phones him to ask about a couple of lawyers. Archie mentions Bill Wengert of the Times on two occasions, and Art Hollis of CBS News once; as best I can remember this is the only time either appears in the Saga. Purley is around, and slightly less hostile than usual: "The attitude of Sergeant Purley Stebbins toward Wolfe and me is yes-and-no, or make it no-but-yes. When he finds us within ten miles of a homicide, he wishes he was on traffic or narcotics, but he knows that something will probably happen that he doesn't want to miss. My attitude toward him is that he could be worse. I could name a few that are." And of course Cramer is here too. "Inspector Cramer of Homicide South has been known to call me Archie. He also has been known to pretend he doesn't remember my name, and that time maybe he really didn't." Cramer shows up at 9:30 in the evening of the day Orrie suicides:

> He always goes straight to the red leather chair, but not that time. Three steps in he stopped and sent his eyes around, left to right then right to left. Then he went to the big globe and turned it, in no hurry, clear around, first to the right and then to the left, while I stood and stared. Then he took off his coat and dropped it on a yellow chair, crossed to the red leather chair, sat, and said, "I've been wanting to do that for years. I don't think I've ever mentioned that it's the biggest and finest globe I ever saw. Also I've never mentioned that this is the best working room I know. The best-looking. I mention it now because I may never see it again."

Because, he means, Wolfe is through in the detective business, and we've already seen Wolfe's reaction to that comment. Later on, Wolfe mentions Cramer's having "whirled" the globe, and Cramer responds, "Goddam it, I didn't whirl it!" But when he gets ready to leave, angry as usual, "he turned, saw the globe, and went and whirled it so hard it hadn't quite stopped when he was through the hall." On Cramer and his cigars: "Cramer got a cigar from a pocket,... stuck it in his mouth and clamped his teeth on it, and took it out again. He hadn't lit one for years"; "Cramer put the cigar between his teeth, took it out, threw it at my wastebasket, and missed by two feet." Finally, the assistant DA this time is Daniel F. Coggin.

PHYSICAL ASPECTS ::: The one-way glass in the front door, which appears in virtually every episode but which I have been ignoring lately, turns out to be larger than I supposed; after Orrie blows himself up Archie says, "There was nothing left of the glass panel in the door, three feet by four feet, but some jagged edges." Archie also tells us that "when someone pushes the button at the front door of the old brownstone, bells ring in four places: in the kitchen, in the office, down in Fritz's room, and up in my room." In the office, the globe has already been mentioned, and here's an item we haven't seen for a while: "the couch, in the corner beyond my desk, was perfectly sleepable, as I knew from experience, having spent quite a few nights on it in emergencies, and on the other side of the projecting wall that made the corner was an equipped bathroom." The "solid gold opener" in Wolfe's drawer gets mentioned, as does "the thin strip of gold he used for a bookmark." Here's something new: Archie says, "I reached to my desk tray, a hollowed-out slab of green marble, for the opener and began to slit." Wolfe tells a third party that "Mr. Goodwin will not use a noiseless typewriter." While using the machine Archie comments: "Much of the room shows in the six-by-four mirror on the wall back of my desk, so I knew I wasn't missing anything while I hit the keys." Archie also mentions "the shelf where we keep the **Times** and the **Gazette** for two weeks." (Wolfe says to Archie, "I keep my copies of the **Times** in my room for a month, as you know.) And he says "one of the bottom shelves had seven directories, not counting the telephone books for the five boroughs and Westchester and Washington, and I had the **Directory of Directors** open to N to see if any of them were on the NATELEC list." One last thing before leaving the office. Archie gives us a diagram of a seating arrangement in the office. Substituting the colors of the chairs for the names of the people in them, here it is:

Wolfe

red

Archie

yellow    yellow    yellow

yellow    yellow

In the kitchen Archie mentions "the little table, and the **Times** was on the rack." When Archie comes down the stairs from his room and reaches the ground floor he "turned right at the bottom instead of left" and he explains that he is going to the kitchen rather than to the office. (This is going to play havoc with my contention that the stairs are at the front of the house. Unless, that is, he is coming down the **back** stairs.) And when Wolfe leaves the office on his way to the elevator he turns right. (Which is okay.) About that elevator, Archie says "it complains more about going down than about going up." Moving up to the second floor, Archie tells us that in Wolfe's room, "of the three windows in the south wall, the two end ones are always open at night about five inches, and the middle one is shut and locked and draped." The fire escape is outside the middle window, and "the fire escape is only a foot wider than the window." Archie, still in Wolfe's room, "got up, went to the phone on the bedstand, switched it on, and dialed." Up now to the third floor: "At the second landing I turned left, swung the door of the South Room open, and turned the light on. I didn't have to check on the bed or towels in the bathroom because I knew everything was in order; all I had to do was turn the radiator on." Now this next thing is peculiar: after installing Pierre in the South Room Archie tells him, "If you open the door and go into the hall before eight o'clock, it will set off a gong in my room and you'll see me coming with guns in both hands." The peculiar thing here is that that alarm system has always before been said to be on **Wolfe's** floor, not Archie's. Archie tells us "There's a shelf of books in my room, my property," and elsewhere he gives us a fuller description of his room's contents: "There were two chairs, a big easy one over by the reading lamp and a small straight one at the little desk." Finally, the plant rooms on the roof: "In the potting room Theodore was sitting at his little desk, writing on his pad of forms, and Wolfe was standing at the long bench, inspecting something in a big pot." And, "Up there, when he sits it's usually on one of the stools at a bench, but there's a chair nearly big enough over in one corner."

ROUTINE AT THE BROWNSTONE ::: When he comes in late at night, Archie says, "I always look in at the office to see if Wolfe has written anything on the pad on my desk." The temperature is kept at seventy degrees while folks are up and about, but at bedtime "we had lowered the thermostat four degrees to save oil." The old chain bolt, much neglected in the past, is damned near worn out from excessive use in this episode. Only once, at 11:10 p.m., does Archie mention the bolt not being on when he gets home; all the other times—at an unspecified time in the afternoon, at a little past eight in the evening, and at 11:30 in the morning are all mentioned—Archie has to ring for Fritz in order to get in. Here's an interesting item on routine: "After lunch you might have thought we were back to normal. Theodore brought down a batch of statistics on germination and performance, and I entered them on the file cards. Week in and week out, that routine, about two percent of which—the few he sells—applies to income and the rest to outgo, takes, on an average, about a third of my time." Archie mentions again his practice of answering the phone "Nero Wolfe's office" before six in the evening, and "Nero Wolfe's residence" after. Wolfe comes down for lunch at 1:15.

ODDS & ENDS ::: Parker has to arrange bail in the amount of $30,000 each for Wolfe and Archie. Archie says that 226 hours elapsed between the time Pierre was blown up and the time Orrie followed him. Here's something interesting:

> I had also done the chores, including drawing a check for three grand for Wolfe to sign because the fifteen hundred had about cleaned out the reserve cash box, and clipping the November 1 coupons from some municipal bonds—in the tidy pile in the upper compartment of the safe with its own lock. I made a face as I clipped, because the rate on those bonds was 5.2 per cent, and high-grade tax-exempt municipals then being issued returned close to 8 per cent. Life is no joke if you're in or above the 50-per-cent bracket, as Wolfe was. Equal to 15 per cent on your money, and you only have to clip coupons—or have Archie Goodwin do it if you're busy nursing orchids.

Lastly, Roman Vilar, of Vilar Associates, a security outfit, tries to hire Wolfe and Archie for his company. It's their names he really wants, so the job would be no more than part time. The pay? Vilar says "the starting figure will be a hundred and twenty thousand for you, ten thousand a month, and thirty-six thousand for Goodwin, three thousand a month." If you have to ask if they accepted the offer, you just haven't been paying attention over the last seventy-odd episodes.

### END OF SAGA

# VLADIMIR GULL
## By Theodore P. Dukeshire

Vladimir Gull is the hero of four books written by Anthony Stuart since 1968. Russian-born Gull "left" for the West during the 1956 Hungarian Revolution. ("Defected," Gull says, is a word the Foreign Office uses.") Now a British subject and on the far side of forty, he makes his living as a free-lance interpreter for the UN and other international organizations.

In his first adventure, *That Man Gull* (English title: *Snap Judgement*), Vladimir is in the interpreters' booth at the UN's Geneva headquarters when, in place of providing a live, verbatim translation of a speech being made by the Russian ambassador, he is forced to read from a document which makes it appear that the U.S. and Russia are going to gang up on China. Determined to find out why, Gull follows a trail which leads to Bucharest and some old friends, not all of whom are glad to see him.

Literally bumping into Diana Hisland, an old girlfriend, doesn't prepare Vladimir for his second adventure, *Vicious Circles*. Gull had almost married Diana before her stern father ("Every Russian's a Communist") broke it up. Now she is governess to a nine-year old count. She and Vladimir plan a trip to Naples, but they have to take the count along when all three are kidnapped by the Red Brigade. They escape easily enough, but Vladimir finds himself accused of engineering the kidnapping, and it's only with the help of Mimi, a Polish Modesty Blaise who likes to wreck bars, that he's able to extricate himself.

Six years ago Vladimir and Miguela Moreno, a Chilean optic designer, had an affair going, but when the Allende regime suddenly collapsed Miguela went back to Chile "to see if she could help in any way." Now, in *Force Play*, she shows up again as a witness for the UN Conference on Human Rights to testify about being held prisoner by the Chilean secret police. She's also terrified of the World Placement Agency, an employment agency which has her booked to go to Prague and seems overly anxious for her to honor her contract. Vladimir tries to help her and in so doing runs afoul of the CIA and another group also interested in the World Agency.

*Midwinter Madness* finds Vladimir on the Channel Island of Guernsey, visiting his pregnant girlfriend's father, Godfrey Mackeson-Beadle. Re-enter Diana Hisland's father, Sir Ronald, who has a wager with Makeson-Beadle that he can hijack some plutonium from a French nuclear plant across the Channel. Vladimir's mirth ends when Hisland's attempt succeeds and the man plans to use the plutonium for the Free Guernsey Movement.

An English newspaper called Vladimir Gull "a rival to James Bond." I agree, and I hope Stuart will keep Vladimir travelling for many more books to come.

# SPY SERIES CHARACTERS IN HARDBACK, II
## By Barry Van Tilburg

DOSSIER #8: Thomas Elphinstone Hambledon.
CREATED BY: Manning Coles.
OCCUPATION: Agent of British Intelligence.
ASSOCIATES: Forgan and Campbell, friends who help him at various times. They actually run a modelmaking shop in London; Inspector Bagshot, a policeman friend that Hambledon works with on home territory.
WEAPONS: Uses revolvers.
OTHER COMMENTS: Drinking, laughing, and in general having a good time while on assignment seem to be Hambledon's forte.

*Drink to Yesterday* (Literary Guild, 1941; Hodder 1941).
*A Toast to Tomorrow* (Literary Guild, 1941; published as *Pray Silence* by Hodder, 1941).
*They Tell No Tales* (Doubleday, 1942; Hodder, 1942).
*Without Lawful Authority* (Doubleday, 1943; Hodder, 1943).
*Green Hazard* (Doubleday, 1945; Hodder, 1945).
*The Fifth Man* (Doubleday, 1946; Hodder, 1946).
*With Intent to Deceive* (Doubleday, 1947; published as *A Bother for Hugh* by Hodder, 1947).
*Let the Tiger Die* (Doubleday, 1947; Hodder 1947).
*Among Those Absent* (Doubleday, 1948; Hodder, 1948).
*Not Negotiable* (Doubleday, 1949; Hodder, 1949).
*Diamonds to Amsterdam* (Doubleday, 1949; Hodder, 1949).
*Dangerous by Nature* (Doubleday, 1950; Hodder, 1950).
*Now or Never* (Doubleday, 1951; Hodder, 1951).
*Night Train to Paris* (Doubleday, 1951; Hodder, 1951).
*Alias Uncle Hugo* (Doubleday, 1952; Hodder, 1952).
*A Knife for the Juggler* (Hodder, 1953; Doubleday, 1964).
*All that Glitters* (Doubleday, 1954; published as *Not for Export* by Hodder, 1954).
*The Man in the Green Hat* (Doubleday, 1955; Hodder, 1955).
*The Basle Express* (Doubleday, 1956; Hodder, 1956).
*Birdwatchers Quarry* (Doubleday, 1956; published as *The Three Beans* by Hodder, 1956).
*Death of an Ambassador* (Doubleday, 1958; Hodder, 1958).
*No Entry* (Doubleday, 1958; Hodder, 1958).
*Concrete Crime* (Doubleday, 1960, published as *Crime in Concrete* by Hodder, 1960).
*Nothing to Declare* (Doubleday, 1960; Hodder, 1960).
*Search for a Sulyan* (Doubleday, 1961; Hodder, 1961).
*The House at Pluck's Gutter* (Hodder, 1963).

DOSSIER #9: Johnny Fedora.
CREATED BY: Desmond Cory.
OCCUPATION: Referred to as a killer for the British Secret Service.
ASSOCIATES: Sebastian Trout, a fellow agent; Jimmy Emerald, another fellow agent; Feramontov, an enemy (Russian) agent that Fedora battles with in the last five books.
WEAPONS: Fedora prefers pistols.
OTHER COMMENTS: During the war and for a short time afterward Fedora was a Nazi hunter. He gave up intelligence work to open a detective agency with Trout and Emerald, only to end up back in the espionage game again.

*Secret Ministry* (Muller, 1951).
*This Traitor, Death* (Muller, 1952).
*Dead Man Falling* (Muller, 1953).
*Intrigue* (Muller, 1954).
*Height of Day* (Muller, 1955).
*High Requiem* (Muller, 1955).
*Johnny Goes North* (Muller, 1956).
*Johnny Goes East* (Muller, 1957).
*Johnny Goes West* (Muller, 1958; Walker, 1967).
*Johnny Goes South* (Muller, 1959; Walker, 1964).
*Undertow* (Muller, 1962; Walker, 1963).
*Hammerhead* (Muller, 1963; published as *Shockwave* by Walker, 1964).
*Feramontov* (Muller, 1966; Walker, 1966).
*Timelock* (Muller, 1967; Walker, 1967).
*Sunburst* (Muller, 1971; Walker, 1971).

DOSSIER #10: Unnamed, called Harry Palmer in the movies.
CREATED BY: Len Deighton.
OCCUPATION: Agent for British Military Intelligence.
ASSOCIATES: Works under Dawlish and Dalby; Colonel Stock of Russian Intelligence is a recurring adversary.
WEAPONS: Can use guns and explosives.
OTHER COMMENTS: Though he has a different name in each book, it is obviously a code name, and the agent is the same one. Michael Caine played Harry Palmer in the movies.
*The Ipcress File* (Cape, 1962; Simon & Schuster, 1963).
*Funeral in Berlin* (Cape, 1964; Putnam, 1965).
*The Billion Dollar Brain* (Cape, 1966; Putnam, 1966).
*An Expensive Place to Die* (Cape, 1967; Putnam, 1967).
*Horse under Water* (Cape, 1968; Putnam, 1968).
*Spy Story* (Cape, 1974; Doubleday, 1976).
*Yesterday's Spy* (Cape, 1975; Doubleday, 1976).
*Catch a Falling Spy* (Doubleday, 1977; published as *Twinkle, Twinkle Little Spy* by Cape, 1976).

DOSSIER #11: Gordon Craigie and Department Z.
CREATED BY: John Creasey.
OCCUPATION: Head of Department Z.
ASSOCIATES: Most of his friends, agents, and assistants get out of the service through death or marriage. Bill Loftus, his second in command, last about the longest.
WEAPONS: Cragie is capable of using a gun.
OTHER COMMENTS: Whereas Creasey's (Gordon Ashe's) Z5 fights on a world-wide basis, Department Z fights mostly on home ground, working closely with the police and the military. Craigie is an ugly little man, but likable and intelligent, and he almost lives in his headquarters.
*The Death Miser* (Melrose, 1932).
*Red Head* (Hurst, 1933).
*First Came a Murder* (Melrose, 1934).
*Death Around the Corner* (Melrose, 1935).
*Mark of the Crescent* (Melrose, 1935).
*Thunder in Europe* (Melrose, 1936).
*The Terror Trap* (Melrose, 1936).
*Carriers of Death* (Melrose, 1937).
*Days of Danger* (Melrose, 1937).
*Death Stands By* (Melrose, 1938).
*Menace* (Long, 1938).

*Murder Must Wait* (Long, 1939).
*Panic* (Long, 1939).
*Death by Night* (Long, 1940)
*The Island of Peril* (Long, 1940).
*Sabotage* (Long, 1941).
*Go Away, Death* (Long, 1941).
*The Day of Disaster* (Long, 1942).
*No Darker Crime* (Stanley Paul, 1943).
*Prepare for Action* (Stanley Paul, 1943).
*Dark Peril* (Stanley Paul, 1944).
*The Peril Ahead* (Long, 1946).
*The Legion of Dark Men* (Stanley Paul, 1947).
*The Department of Death* (Evans, 1949).
*The Enemy Within* (Evans, 1950).
*Dead or Alive* (Evans, 1951).
*A Kind of Prisoner* (Evans, 1954).
*The Black Spiders* (Hodder, 1957).

DOSSIER #12: Dennis Tyler.
CREATED BY: Diplomat (John Franklin Carter).
OCCUPATION: Chief of the Bureau of Current Political Intelligence.
ASSOCIATES: His wife, Cynthia.
WEAPONS: Pistols.
OTHER COMMENTS: Tyler investigates murders with political ramifications. They seem to be his favorite hobby.
*Murder in the State Department* (Cape, 1930).
*Murder in the Embassy* (Cape, 1930; Harrap, 1932).
*Scandal in the Chancery* (Cape, 1931).
*The Corpse on the White House Lawn* (Covici, 1932; Hurst, 1933).
*Death in the Senate* (Covici, 1933).
*Slow Death at Geneva* (Coward, 1934).
*The Brain Trust Murder* (Coward, 1935).

DOSSIER #13: Brian "Boysie" Oakes.
CREATED BY: John Gardner
OCCUPATION: Liquidating Agent for British Sepecial Security.
ASSOCIATES: Col. Mostyn, his boss, and Charlie Griffin, a hired killer.
WEAPONS: Boysie shies away from most any weapon.
OTHER COMMENTS: Boysie is the kind of person that if he fell into a mudpuddle someone would likely step over him instead of help him. He is either afraid or allergic to everything imaginable. The most comical book in the series has to be *Traitor's Exit*, in which Boysie runs away from the opposition, leading a merry chase in a clown's car. Anyone who has ever seen a circus clown's car knows what I mean. Boysie's idiocy was brought to life in the movies by Rod Taylor.
*The Liquidator* (Muller, 1964; Viking, 1964).
*Understrike* (Muller, 1965; Viking, 1965).
*Amber Nine* (Muller, 1966; Viking, 1966).
*Madrigal* (Muller, 1968; Viking, 1968).
*Founder Member* (Muller, 1969).
*Traitor's Exit* (Muller, 1970).
*The Airline Pirates* (Muller, 1970; published as *Air Apparent* by Putnam, 1971).
*Killer for a Song* (Hodder, 1975).

DOSSIER #14: James Bond (007).
CREATED BY: Ian Fleming.
CONTINUED BY: Robert Markham (Kingsley Amis), Christopher Wood.
OCCUPATION: A licensed-to-kill agent of Her Majesty's Secret Service.
ASSOCIATES: "M" (Miles Masservy), his boss; "Q", maker of gadgets and special equipment; Felix Leiter, a friend who worked for CIA and FBI before getting retired because a shark ate him; Miss Moneypenny, secretary to "M"; Ernst Blofeld, a recurring adversary; Spectre, an international criminal organization; Smersh, the dreaded Russian assassination arm of Intelligence.
WEAPONS: Started out using a Beretta .25 but later changed to a Walther PPK. Also uses the gadgets that "Q" comes up with.
OTHER COMMENTS: James Bond is the most talked about and written about secret agent in the history of the genre. Even though his creator has died Bond still lives on in other books. Bond has been brought to life in the movies by Sean Connery, George Lazenby and Roger Moore. I think Connery fit the part better. Imagine him fifty pounds lighter, with a scar running down his cheek.

*Casino Royale* (Cape, 1950; MacMillan, 1953).
*Live and Let Die* (Cape, 1954; MacMillan, 1954).
*Moonraker* (Cape, 1955); MacMillan, 1955).
*Diamonds Are Forever* (MacMillan, 1956).
*From Russia With Love* (Cape, 1957; MacMillan, 1957).
*Doctor No* (MacMillan, 1958).
*Goldfinger* (MacMillan, 1960).
*Thunderball* (MacMillan, 1960; Cape, 1961).
*For Your Eyes Only* (Cape, 1960; Viking, 1960).
*The Spy Who Loved Me* (Cape, 1960; Viking, 1961).
*On Her Majesty's Secret Service* (Cape, 1963; New American Library, 1963).
*You Only Live Twice* (Cape, 1964; New American Library, 1964).
*The Man With the Golden Gun* (Cape, 1965; New American Library, 1965).
*Octopussy* (New American Library, 1966).
*Colonel Sun*, by Robert Markham (Cape, 1967; Harper & Row, 1968).
*Property of a Lady* (Treasury of Modern Mystery, Doubleday, 1973).
*James Bond, the Spy Who Loved Me*, by Christopher Wood (Cape, 1977).
*James Bond and Moonraker*, by Christopher Wood (Cape, 1979).

DOSSIER #15: Quiller
CREATED BY: Adam Hall (Elleston Trevor).
OCCUPATION: Agent of British Intelligence.
ASSOCIATES: Loman, a controller; Parkis, a controller; Egerton, a controller; Tilson, a controller.
WEAPONS: Hates guns and says once you use them you tend to depend too much upon them.
OTHER COMMENTS: Quiller is what I call a professional survivor. His controllers throw him into a situation and expect him to survive. He was brought to life in the movies by George Segal and on television by Michael Jayston.

*The Quiller Memorandum* (Simon & Schuster, 1965; published as *The Berlin Memorandum* by Collins, 1965).

*The 9th Directive* (Simon & Schuster, 1967; Collins, 1967).
*The Striker Portfolio* (Simon & Schuster, 1968; Collins, 1968).
*The Warsaw Document* (Doubleday, 1971).
*The Tango Briefing* (Doubleday, 1973).
*The Mandarin Cypher* (Doubleday, 1975).
*The Kobra Manifesto* (Doubleday, 1976).
*The Sinkiang Executive* (Doubleday, 1978).
*The Scorpion Signal* (Doubleday, 1980).

DOSSIER #16: Col. Charles Russell.
CREATED BY: William Haggard (Richard Henry Clayton).
OCCUPATION: Head of British Intelligence (later retired).
ASSOCIATES: No regulars.
WEAPONS: Mostly uses his brains.
OTHER COMMENTS: Russell is a very easy-going person who copes extremely well with various situations. He is in control at all times.
*Slow Burner* (Cassell, 1958; Little, Brown, 1958).
*Venetian Blind* (Cassell, 1959; Washburn, 1959).
*The Arena* (Washburn, 1961).
*The Unquiet Sleep* (Washburn, 1962).
*The High Wire* (Cassell, 1963; Washburn, 1963).
*The Antagonists* (Cassell, 1964; Washburn, 1964).
*The Powder Barrell* (Cassell, 1965; Washburn, 1965).
*The Hard Sell* (Cassell, 1965; Washburn, 1966).
*The Power House* (Cassell, 1966; Washburn, 1967).
*The Conspirators* (Cassell, 1967; Walker, 1968).
*A Cool Day for a Killing* (Cassell, 1968; Walker, 1969).
*The Hardliners* (Cassell, 1970; Walker, 1970).
*The Bitter Harvest* (Cassell, 1971; Walker, 1971).
*The Old Masters* (Cassell, 1973; Walker, 1973).
*Scorpion's Tail* (Cassell, 1975; Walker, 1975).
*Yesterday's Enemies* (Cassell, 1976; Walker, 1976).
*The Poison People* (Cassell, 1977; Walker, 1977).
*Visa to Limbo* (Cassell, 1978; Walker, 1978).
*The Median Line* (Cassell, 1979).

DOSSIER #17: George Smiley.
CREATED BY: John LeCarre (David Cornwell).
OCCUPATION: Agent (later Head) of British Intelligence department called "Circus".
ASSOCIATES: Lady Ann Sercombe, his wife; Connie Sachs, head of research; Alec Leamas, an agent; Peter Guillam, an agent; Karla, a recurring enemy (Smiley's Russian opposite).
WEAPONS: Prefers pistols.
OTHER COMMENTS: Smiley has been described as a short, squat toad. He truly seems to enjoy the game. Even though he retired, he did return. James Mason played Smiley in the movies.
*Call for the Dead* (Gollancz, 1961; Walker, 1962).
*A Murder of Quality* (Gollancz, 1962; Walker, 1963).
*The Spy Who Came in from the Cold* (Gollancz, 1963; Coward, 1963).
*The Looking Glass War* (Gollancz, 1965; Coward, 1965).
*Tinker, Tailor, Soldier, Spy* (Knopf, 1974; Hodder, 1974).
*The Honourable Schoolboy* (Knopf, 1977; Hodder, 1977).
*Smiley Goes Home* (The Bell House Book, Hodder, 1979).
*Smiley's People* (Knopf, 1980; Hodder, 1980).

DOSSIER #18: Paul Chavasse.
CREATED BY: Martin Fallon (Harry Patterson).
OCCUPATION: Agent for Her Majesty's Secret Service.
ASSOCIATES: The Chief, his boss.
WEAPONS: Prefers his hands or a pistol.
OTHER COMMENTS: The books are very violent; Chavasse enjoys killing. He says that if he were to have been German in World War II he probably would have worked for the SS.

*The Testament of Caspar Schultz* (Abelard, 1962).
*Year of the Tiger* (Abelard, 1963).
*The Keys of Hell* (Abelard, 1965).
*Midnight Never Comes* (John Long, 1965).
*The Dark Side of the Street* (John Long, 1967).
*A Find Night for Dying* (John Long, 1969).

# LOOKING FOR RACHEL WALLACE AND GINGER NORTH
## By George Kelley

Recently, I read Robert B. Parker's *Looking for Rachel Wallace* (Delacorte, 1980) and John Dunning's *Looking for Ginger North* (Fawcett, 1980). Beyond the similar titles, both books involve a search, but what they find makes one book a shabby writing exercise and the other a minor masterpiece.

I've admired the first few cases of Parker's Boston-based private eye, Spenser. The books had a tough, lean style with original characters and nifty prose. But Spenser's fallen on hard times in *Promised Land, The Judas Goat,* and now *Looking for Rachel Wallace*. Spenser's gotten flabby. He's got a girldfriend/lover who raises his conscience about women's rights and equality. It's as if Sam Spade took up with Gloria Steinem. Spenser's ego grows. Too much of *Looking for Rachel Wallace* is preoccupied with shoddy psychoanalysis. Here's a typical conversation with Spenser, Spenser's girlfriend Susan, and Rachel Wallace—the radical lesbian feminist Spenser's hired to protect:

> "Why do you engage in things that are violent and dangerous?" Rachel asked.
> "... Well," I said, "the violence is a kind of side-effect, I think. I have always wanted to live life on my own terms. And I have always tried to do what I can do. I am good at certain kinds of things; I have tried to go in that direction."
> "The answer doesn't satisfy me," Rachel said.
> "It doesn't have to. It satisfies me."
> "What he won't say," Susan said, "and what he may not even admit to himself is that he'd like to be Sir Gawain. He was born five hundred years too late. If you understand that, you understand most of what you are asking."
> "Six hundred years," I said. [p. 25]

Heavy stuff. So Spenser thinks he's a knight in slightly tarnished white armor. And sure enough, Rachel fires him, and sure enough, Rachel gets kidnapped.

Spenser, like the knight he imagines himself to be, solves the case and rushes to Rachel's rescue. No surprises here as we have a mawkish rescue scene:

> Tears began to run down Rachel's face, and I put my arms around her, and she cried. And I cried. In between crying I said, "I got you. I got you."
> She didn't say anything. [p. 203]

This drippy farce is low on action and high on Parker's concept of "realism". Unfortunately, Parker's writing talents have deteriorated to the point where his book's plot doesn't hang together and all the intense dialogues on social awareness remain flat and phony and boring.

John Dunning's *Looking for Ginger North* is an infinitely better book that Parker's fiasco.

Dunning opens with Wes Harrison, a race track drifter, becoming more than a piece of human jetsam. Harrison, an orphan, is a man with a quest similar to the lead character in P. D.

James's *Innocent Blood* (Scribner's, 1980): to find his parents, and failing that, to find out *about* them.

Following slender clues, Harrison drifts across America until he reaches Pacifica, California. Finally, he finds a lead during a poker game:

> "Ginger North," Poole said.... "Wasn't she the dippy bitch who killed herself thirty years ago?"
> "... What was she to you, anyway?" Grayson said.
> I looked from face to face. Even Charlie had stopped grinning and was hanging close, waiting.
> "That dippy bitch was my mother," I said. [p. 30]

Harrison becomes obsessed with his mother's death, with the strange and terrible events of thirty years ago. And his search for the answers leads to the murder of an innocent man sleeping in Harrison's bed.

The violence escalates as Harrison comes closer and closer to the truth hidden by thirty years of lies, and the conclusion hits you with jarring power. *Looking for Ginger North* is one of the year's superior mysteries; John Dunning is a writer to watch.

And if you're looking for a good book to read, forget about Rachel Wallace, and join Wes Harrison, looking for Ginger North.

# IT'S ABOUT CRIME

## Notes on Current Reading

### By Marvin Lachman

It may be unpatriotic to say so, but for me the *real* American revolution began in 1967. That was the year the deluge of writing *about* crime fiction began with TAD and *The Mystery Reader's Newsletter*. Since then, there have been dozens of books of biography, criticism, analysis, and history—all about our favorite genre. Journals have come and gone, but TAD is still here, and *The MYSTERY FANcier*, *The Poisoned Pen*, *Mystery*, *DAPA-EM*, *The Not So Private Eye*, etc., are all welcome additions to the fold and indicate there is no end in sight. Of recent books, representing great variety, the most interesting is John Nieminski's *The Saint Magazine Indes* (published by Cook-McDowell Publications, copies available from Mr. Nieminski, 2848 Western, Park Forest, IL 60466 at $6.75). It is an alphabetical listing of every story, author, and series character to appear in that now-defunct magazine from 1953 to 1967. Read some of the names of authors whose work was published there (e.g., Ambler, Fredric Brown, Leo Bruce, Joseph Conrad, B. Traven, Helen Reilly, Harlan Ellison, John Jakes) and then weep that you and I, unlike John, were not smart enough to collect a complete run.

The mystery field has become so "respectable" that *Murder Ink* was a best-selling trade paperback late in 1977. Now, there is an affirmative action sequel, *Murderess Ink* (Workman Publishing Co., $6.95), again perpetrated by Dilys Winn. Some of the true crime material may be of only marginal interest to fans of mystery fiction, though Mary Groff's article on "lady killers" is alone worth the cost of the book. There are more errors in *Murderess Ink* than I recall in its predecessor, e.g.:

1. Elizabeth Linington, as Lesley Egan, writes about Vic Varallo, not Vatallo.
2. Rinehart's Miss Pinkerton never appeared in twenty novels, only two, in fact.
3. Phyllis Bentley's Miss Phipps is English, not American.
4. Wade Miller's book about a strip teaser is *Deadly Weapon*, not *Dead Weapons*.
5. The picture on page 285 is of Margaret Lockwood, not Madeleine Carroll.

Errors aside, there is still much that is very enjoyable here, including biographical sketches, dozens of pictures, and a marvelous translation of British crime slang for U.S. readers. Miss Winn, is it true your next book will be about crime writers in part of Asia and will be called *India Ink*?

Frederick Ungar Publishing Co., 250 Park Avenue South, New York, NY 10003, is responsible for two of the recent nonfiction books. The less unusual of them is *The Bedside, Bathtub, and Armchair Companion to Agatha Christie*, $9.95, edited by Dick Riley and Pam McAllister. It is at least the fourth recent book to list all of her mysteries and the third to give brief synopses of her plots. While, like its predecessors, it lists all of her short stories, it too does not give the original date and location of publication. *That* would have been a research breakthrough. Still, it is an enjoyable book and a splendid gift for Christie fans. It is illustrated with dozens of paperback covers and includes cross word puzzles, quotations, and articles about her films and plays. Not novel, but nice.

David Geherin's *Sons of Sam Spade*, $9.95 from Ungar, is a greatly expanded version of his article in TAD, volume 11, number 1. Mr. Geherin, an Associate Professor of English at Eastern Michigan University, discusses three very contemporary authors and their private detectives: Robert B. Parker and Spenser; Andrew Bergman and Levine; and Roger Simon and Moses Wine. The biographical data about the authors is new and interesting. While plots are discussed in too much detail, and there is too much striving for effect, e.g., clever variations on Wine's name, these faults are more than balanced by some really good insights into how the Private Eye novel has evolved.

There is an encouraging recent revival in the classical detective story. Zebra Books is emphasizing the idea of giving the readers a chance to guess the solutions using traditional verbal clues plus visual clues (a cover picture and drawings within). Their appeal is expressly to women. All detectives are female, and Zebra begins its advertisement of titles on the last page of each book with the line, "Every woman needs a little mystery in her life." One of their recent titles, Norma Schier's *Death Goes Skiing*, is a well-plotted, readable mystery in her series about attorney Kay Barth. The skiing scenes are good, especially a climactic blizzard, and the setting of Aspen Colorado seems authentically realized. Some of the pictures are irrelevant, but others do permit deduction and, thus, add to the grand game between author and reader. However, I suggest that the people at Zebra Books reconsider their policy of excluding the male half of their potential readership.

That old staple of mysteries geared to women, the elderly widow/spinster, is back in *Dead to Rites* (Penguin, 1978) by Sylvia Angus. Mrs. Wagstaff, a Rinehart character brought into the 1970's, is sentimental, but she is also physically and mentally tough. *Dead to Rites* is adequately plotted but greatly enhanced by its unusual setting, the Mayan ruins at Chichén Itzá in Yucatan, Mexico. Having visited there four years ago, I can subscribe to her authenticity, right up to the excruciating steepness of the pyramid steps.

It is understandable, but sad, that so many writers go downhill near the ends of their careers and, like ball players, do not retire in time. Dorothy L. Sayers was one of the few to stop writing when she was at her peak. Christie, Gardner, and Queen, on the other hand, had last books that were embarrassing. I fear that Ngaio Marsh may follow their pattern. I have read all thirty of her Roderick Alleyn novels, and the latest, *Grave Mistake* (1978), reprinted by Jove, is the worst. The writing is civilized and sophisticated, but it does not compensate for uninspired plotting and very little action—physical or cerebral. I hope Dame Ngaio, who has provided me with so many pleasant hours, has a few good books left.

June Thomson is a British writer who is being touted as one of the future greats in the field. Bantam has recently reprinted three of her books, *Death Cap, A Question of Identity*, and *The Habit of Loving*, all of which I hope to read soon. Perhaps reading them will answer the question of why her series character, Inspector Finch, became Inspector Rudd when her books were published in the United States. The only explanation I can think of is to avoid confusion with another fictional detective, Inspector Septimus Finch, but Margaret Erskine's series character is far better known in England than in the U.S.

Praise be to the publishers who do not let old classics die. Avon has been reprinting the Patrick Quentin series about Peter and Iris Duluth. I readily admit that I could not finish the two books upon which the series built its reputation: *Puzzle for Fools* (1936) and *Puzzle for Players* (1938), but I plan to try them again. On the other hand, the third book about the Duluths, *Puzzle for Puppets* (1944) is one of my favorite books, with its breakneck pace, calculated lunacy, and San Francisco-during-World War II setting.

Who would ever have expected a legend, *The Floating Admiral*, to be reprinted in popular paperback format? Charter did it, and they deserve the immediate support of all aficionados. Who can resist a novel that has an introduction by Sayers and was written, a chapter apiece, by the members of London's Detection Club: Chesterton, Wade, Christie, Rhode, Knox, Crofts, Berkeley, et al.

Although its reprints are not old enough to be real classics, the latest issue of *Ellery Queen's Anthology* (Spring-Summer 1980, $2.25, from Davis Publications, 380 Lexington Avenue, New York, NY 10017) contains an excellent assortment from the recent past. There is Rex Stout's "Eeny Meeny Murder Mo" (1962), one of the best Nero Wolfe novelets, and Patricia McGerr's "Hid-and-Seek—Russian Style", which I found to be the best piece of new short fiction published in EQMM during 1976. Add twenty more stories, and you have an uncommon bargain.

William Oscar Johnson's *The Zero Factor*, just published by Pocket Books, Inc., owes nothing to the past as a mystery, but everything to American history, and the much publicized fact that our last seven presidents, beginning with Lincoln in 1860, who were elected in years ending in zero did not leave the White House alive. This macabre tradition becomes an obsession with Augustus York, elected in 1980, who seems at the mercy of crazed gunmen, a professional assassin, and even a drunk driver. Unlike most of the proliferation of White House fiction of recent years, *Zero* is plausible and provides some genuine insights to the office, including the tremendous strain it places on the occupant. It also tells a cracking good story, with an exciting climax.

# MYSTERY*FILE

## Short Reviews by Steve Lewis

Robert B. Parker. *Looking for Rachel Wallace.* Delacorte Press, 1980, 219 pp., $8.95.

    As Parker's hero of long standing, and as a private eye possessing some amount of character, Spenser is often called upon to justify himself. What his reply usually boils down to is that he is who he is, and that he does what he does because he likes it, and because he's good at it.
    Not that everyone always agrees. Rachel Wallace is a lesbian writer and a radical feminist. She sees cops, for example, and in her own words, as agents of repression, end quote, but she does need a bodyguard. Her latest book is overtly controversial. Her publisher hires Spenser. He looks and acts like everything Rachel Wallace hates. She fires him. She's kidnapped.
    He rescues her, an act of violence straight from the Mickey Spillane handbook of reputation and revenge, but an action tempered and highlighted by the sharp, biting overtones of a fine post-graduate education in social philosophy. Rachel Wallace is placed in a quandary. Spenser (figuratively) shrugs it off. He enjoys his male adolescent fantasy role-playing, and even while recognizing it for what it is, there is still more than a fifty-fifty chance that you will too. You may even agree with me that this is one of the better books of the year, so far, in or out of the detective field.
    And even if you don't, if you like your mystery fiction filled with action as well as more than a touch of character, you'll still probably read this one all the way through in a single sitting. (A)* (*Reviews so marked have appeared earlier in the Hartford *Courant*.)

Ruth Rendell. *Means of Evil.* Doubleday, 1979, first U.S. edition 1980, 176 pp., $8.95.

    In Rendell's opening note she implies that each of these five stories, two published here for the first time, could easily be considered a novel in itself, in miniature, so to speak. Her Inspector Wexford, a grandfather now, is the only person who appears in all five, but in four of them many of the same familiar faces of family, friends and assorted villians of Kingsmarkham keep returning.
    Not surprisingly, Wexford himself emerges as the most human of this large cast of characters. The others suffer too greatly from the abrupt transitions between scenes, inadequately paved over by awkward-sounding dialogue. Writing in the short form, Rendell also seems overly fond of encyclopedic gimmickry rather than more subtle means of conveying information to the reader. While overall these stories are better by far than average, in my opinion they still rate a notch lower than the work the author does when she takes the amount of space she needs to properly express herself. (B)*

Marian Babson. *Murder, Murder, Little Star.* Walker, 1977, first U.S. edition 1980, 177 pp., $9.95.

Back thirty or forty years ago, screwball Hollywood murder mysteries were all the rage. Today, except for a few rundown private eyes who still put in appearances now and then for old times' sake, the territory has been all but abandoned.

But not quite. Recently there was George Baxt's "The Neon Graveyard," but that overextravaganza was a huge sorry flop, better forgotten. It's evidently been left up to an English-woman† to show us that there's still life in the old scenario of murder on the set. Here she writes of a ten-year-old moppet named Twinkle, whose temper can be best compared to a delicate case of dynamite. Filming overseas may be cheaper, but it's certainly no less dangerous.

Cliches abound, to be sure, but with Babson's smooth writing style and her indominable sense of fun, plus a few serious moments as well, they do go down easily. The murder is more accidental than not, however, and unfortunately its solution comes too much from nowhere in particular. (C plus)*

Bill Granger. *Public Murders*. Jove Y5130, 1980, 275 pp.; $1.95.

The stage for this hard-bitten police procedural is the city of Chicago, the villain a crazed rapist-murderer who kills his first victim in Grant Park in broad daylight. This is the truth—this is not the sanitized Dell Shannon version of cops and robbers. The police and the district attorney's staff are sweating, fear-ridden, and real. Equating justice in Chicago to the judicial system, we get a sweltering mass of humanity to be processed. In search of the truth, we get the shit side of Chicago politics, and the scum of Chicago nightlife. The American way consists of fast bureaucratic footwork, spreading the heat around, and dedication (in some quarters) above and beyond the call of duty.

Piece by piece, everything is here. Overall the pace is too uneven and low-keyed for this book to have succeeded as a hardcover bestseller. There've been too many books telling similar stories for it to have been noticed in paperback. Do you ever get the feeling that nothing ever works? Read this. (B)

Colin Dexter. *Service of All the Dead*. St. Martin's, 1979, first U.S. edition 1980, 256 pp., $9.95.

Instead of serenity and Christian fellowship, all that Detective Chief Inspector Morse uncovers in the Oxfordian parish of St. Frideswide's is bitter hatred and blood-letting violence. With all but two of the participants of the opening prologue flung out of towers or otherwise eventually done away with, spotting the identity of the killer does not immediately seem to be that much of a problem.

Keep in mind, however, that upmost and foremost this is a puzzle story. Working a mixed combination of straightforward detection and the omniscient eye of third person singular and plural, Dexter nevertheless manages the unexpected, a twist or

---

†I hate to admit it, but I guess it sometimes pays to read the blurbs on the back jacket flaps. Marian Babson is not English by birth, but hails instead from right here in New England. A solid background like that never fails to show.

two in this—how else to say it?--this loudly-sung paean to the twisted corridors of ulterior human behavior. (B minus)*

Phyllis Swan. *Find Sherri!* Leisure #641, 1979; 208 pp.; $1.75.

    Private eyes and runaway children have a natural affinity for each other. Sherri, of course, is the kid who can't be found. Anna Jugedinski is the private eye who's hired by Sherri's grandmother to find her.
    Right. No kidding. A polish private eye. Not a glamorous one. She's trying to eke out a living in the same slum-like neighborhood she grew up in, in the heart of her hometown of St. Mary's most rundown district. Some of her childhood friends are now on the other side of the law. She's trying to make sure that the teenage brother who lives with her does not follow in their footsteeps. She's in love with her long-time benefactor, Mike Roark, shief of police, who's married and has another woman on the side. Anna was raped by Angelo Amarosa when she was thirteen, and she has not allowed another man to touch her since. Angelo Amarosa also seems to know where Sheri is today.
    Otherwise she has no problems.
    This is not, repeat not, a mere ethnic excuse for a detective novel. Anna begins the story already a fully developed character, and the gradually revealed story of her life seems to slow the story down not one bit. Some vicious undertones emerge as the limits of the case she is working on widen as expected, and the pressures on her increase. As a whole the book is a little rough around the edges, and the flock of characters in Anna Jugedinski's life can get to be a little confusing, but she has now become a series character. The second and third volumes of her adventures have already appeared. I'm going to read them. (B)

A. B. Guthrie, Jr. *No Second Wind.* Houghton Mifflin, 1980; 216 pp.; $9.95.

    Just as novels about science and scientists are seldom considered science fiction, even without a properly conceived definition of the matter, there is an equally large distinction between the category of fiction called "westerns" and what can only be termed novels of the West. What the distinction is, and where exactly the borderline falls, is hard to say. Whatever and wherever, A. B. Guthrie, Jr., author of such books as *The Big Sky* and *The Way West*, writes the latter. Novels of the West.
    Even when his works come published and packaged subtly disguised as mystery fiction. This is the third adventure, so far, of Sheriff Chick Charleston, guardian of law and order in modern-day Midbury, Montana. The story takes place when the temperature is a snowless forty below, but tempers are slowly boiling over. Outside of town a group of miners encamped in trailers wait not-so-patiently for an all-clear on a proposed strip-mining operation. On the other hand, this is cattle country, and most of the local ranchers are vociferously against it, and them.
    Charleston's county consists of 2294 square miles of lonesome countryside, and this is what Guthrie is also writing about. From his typewriter comes beautifully sharp vignette

characterizations of men unafraid of nature--nor of other men, for that matter. (B plus)*

Stanton Forbes. *The Will and Last Testament of Constance Cobble.* Doubleday (Crime Club), 1980; 178 pp.; $7.95.

There is a subcategory of mystery fiction, albeit a small one, that insists upon incestuously concerning itself with, you guessed it, mystery fiction. Take the example undoubtedly most familiar to everyone, the case of the continuing adventures of Ellery Queen. Now, as you probably already know, Ellery Queen, the character, is a mystery writer. As such he happens to solve detective stories as well, and he does very nicely at it, too. But, wait, there's more. The stories *about* Ellery Queen were written *by* Ellery Queen, another writer altogether, in the real world two cousins from Brooklyn who grew up together and who spent their lives writing together under that peculiarly fine-sounding pseudonym. And a more tangled web of intrigue than this it would take a Hercule Poirot to unravel!

But there's the point. It did not take long in the relatively short history of detective and mystery fiction before mystery writers began to find themselves the detective heroes in the stories of others. They've been victims as well, too many times to count, and they've been villains too. And in this, the latest of the many mystery thrillers written by Stanton Forbes, one Constance Cobble manages to make herself at least two out of the three. More than that, I will not say.

It is safe to say that Mrs. Cobble is a mystery writer. Works of fiction are usually intended to be a mirror of sorts upon the real world, but somehow her latest novel almost too successfully begins to reflect the characters surrounding her in the small Caribbean island of St. Martin, and the events taking place there. The chief example has become the drowning of Pauline Grey in Constance Cobble's current work-in-progress, closely paralleled by the subsequent real-life death of one Bootsie Baker. Mrs. Cobble, a widow, takes her characters from real life, a bit here, a piece there, but suddenly reality seems to be mocking her.

Science fiction enthusiasts, I suspect, are going to find the edges of the two stories, blurred between fact and fantasy, easire to keep clear in their minds. There are times when Constance Cobble seems to have slipped completely into the world she has created, but then again, all successful writers do this to some extent, don't they?

As the real author, Stanton Forbes agrees with my own pet theory that it is the people who make the story, even in a mystery novel--yes, even more than the puzzle itself. People confronted with the puzzle, with other people, with their own emotions. This time, regrettably, with the constant switching from one story to the other, the one actually inside the other, the characterizations have come out distantly and subtly out of focus, as if the reader were forced to look constantly through the wrong end of a loosely-mounted telescope. Otherwise here is what would certainly have been one of the mystery novels of the year--of many years, for that matter.

It is a valiant effort, nonetheless, and most certainly it is worth reading. In fact, for its incidental view into the internal workings of the detective story writer's mind, this has to be considered required reading for anyone who has ever seriously considered writing a mystery story him- or herself, but who hasn't, at least not yet.

So here's an exercise for the reader. The ending is subject to some immediate puzzlement and then some possible misunderstanding. Read it and then decide--and you can also take this as a dare if you want to--how would you have filled in the blank? (B plus)*

Stanley Ellin. *Star Light Star Bright*. Ballantine #28541-7, 1979, 1980; 185 pp.; $1.95.

Ellen tries, but he just can't convince me that Johnny Milano is the tough private detective that everybody else seems to think he is. And then again, it's probably safe to say that this wasn't exactly what Ellin had in mind to begin with. Milano overpowers a disgruntled fence on page one, but then he makes a comment about Marcel Proust a few pages down the road, and that's when you should realize that something a little out of the ordinary is going on.

Now, an attempt at something like a little characterization, while it may not shake the world too greatly, couldn't possibly hurt the traditional private eye novel--could it?

An old girl friend, an ex-movie actress whom Milano helped out of a jam three years ago, is in trouble again. Her new husband, who is rich, calls Milano for help. For money, and not for sentimental reasons, Milano takes the job. Someone is threatening the life of Mr. Quist's religious and spiritual mentor. He has already killed her husband's dog.

Milano does have a mean streak, and it arises occasionally as the need arises. He's also the sort of Travis McGee listener to whom women always end up telling their life stories. As such, he also seems to be a qualified sex-therapist, and a once-satisfied customer apparently wants to come back for more.

Once or twice Ellen seems to be guilty of sloppy timetabling, which is surprising, since his stories are always so meticulously told, but he winds it all up with a smashing, suspenseful ending that, if you've been snoozing, will take you completely by surprise.

Overall, a smooth professional job by a writer who knows how to write. And as a bonus, he's come up with a brand new theory that connects Jack the Ripper with Vincent van Gogh. He tosses it in for free. (B plus)

Bill Pronzini. *Labyrinth*. St. Martin's, 1980; 186 pp.; $8.95.

While the number of hardcover mysteries being published by some companies is holding firm, cutbacks in detective fiction elsewhere are being made left and right. High prices, cuts in library budgets, lack of customer demand for hardcover fiction in general, all seem to be contributors. It's difficult to keep old favorites from popping up somewhere, however, and in the past couple of weeks it's been good to welcome a couple of them back.

After four books at Random House, a decreased emphasis there on mystery fiction has forced Bill Pronzini's unnamed pulp-collecting detective to switch his sleuthing adventures over to St. Martin's Press. The gain is both St. Martin's, most of whose detective output before now has been reprinted from England, and ours. The pulp magazines are gone, and their many quaint action-oriented characters--but not their effervescent flavor, not as long as writers like Pronzini deliberately keep their memory and colorful traditions alive in books like this one.

His detective without a name is fiftyish, out of shape, maybe even a slob on the surface, but you get the impression that being a private eye is the only thing in life he'd ever consider doing.

A young college coed is murdered, and she has his card in her purse. The man he is hired to protect from himself is blamed for the shooting of another man instead, and the second man happens to be the father of the dead girl's fiance, who has disappeared. The maze of circumstances that connects the two cases is paved with coincidence, but it's coincidence that's been well-planned in advance for.

The mood is often darkly sombre, the deadly nighttime swim in Bodega Bay is tense and suspenseful, and I'll lay odds that you'll find that Pronzini has set you up again for a surprise in the next-to-the-last chapter with clues you never even spotted. Of all the private investigator series being written today, this one is probably the one most fun to read. (B plus)*

John Ball. *Then Came Violence.* Doubleday (Crime Club), 1980; 208 pp.; $8.95.

Another sleuth who's also just changed publishers has a name known to millions, thanks to Sidney Portier's superb movie impersonation of Pasadena's crack police detective, Virgil Tibbs. The last few Tibbs novels have come from Little, Brown, but Crime Club's got him now, and this first one from the folks at Doubleday is a fine one.

The question immediately facing the reader is what the connection between the armed robbery of a small neighborhood grocery store and the imminent collapse of a newly independent African nation can possibly be. Not only does Virgil Tibbs gain a new family from this diplomatic crisis, the protective custody of the beautiful wife and two young children of Bakara's besieged president, but on another front he's charged with uncovering a gang of vigilantes apparently intent on righting all the wrongs committed by California's overly lenient judicial system.

A great deal of Portier seems to have crept into Ball's view of his own hero, or was it just ideal casting to begin with? Tibbs is a very formal man in both attitude and behavior, but he is a stalwart friend to have and a person of iron control. It's easy to see him as Ball would have you at one point, a pillar of decency in a world awash in violence.

The two stories eventually come smashingly together, but Tibbs thankfully manages to keep his cool. Ball is a better writer than average, and this story is chillingly good. It's designed to grab you and not let you go, and it succeeds on both counts. (A)*

Michael Geller. *A Corpse for a Candidate.* Belmont Tower #51478, 1980; 190 pp.; $1.75.

This is #2 in the Bud Dugan series. I missed the first one, an opus entitled *Mahem on the Coney Island Beat.* Perhaps you saw it, but if not, in this one Dugan was apparently busted from detective in the NYPD to a patrolman before getting a chance to redeem himself. In this one he's been promoted to the city's special Crime Priority Unit, which specializes in crimes of especially sensitive natures.

Which obviously has to include the murder of Amanda Mellis, leading candidate for the job of mayor. Running against her is a radical black named Fullerton Mack. And not only was Amanda forcibly eliminated from the race, there is evidence to suggest that she was probably raped as well.

Dugan likes his job, even though he's forced to learn the rops of political infighting in a hurry. While the solution of the mystery comes far to abruptly, it is the climax of a staggering one-two-three punch of powerful political revelations. After that, the ending is a letdown, the remaining pages being filled by nothing more than a perfectly ordinary action thriller.

Dugan, as it turns out, is a lousy judge of character. Nor is he himself a strong enough character for the decision he makes in the final chapter to be more than remotely believable. Either that, or he's a stronger character than I thought he was. (C)

Hugh Pentecost. *Beware Young Lovers*. Dodd Mead, 1980; 176 pp. $7.95.

Here's the inside scoop on the latest murder to take place in Pierre Chambrun's otherwise smoothly operating Hotel Beaumont. Don't worry, though. Pentecost is more concerned with the movie and television business, the real story, than he is about the more mundane headaches involved in running a huge modern-day lodging-house.

Outside the hotel the latest in a series of young male companions of an aging movie actress is found murdered. Her previous such paramour disappeared without a trace three years before. The only connection seems to be "The Dick Thomas Show," a Merv Griffin type of operation now set up for taping in the Beaumont.

Pentecost knows the kind of dirt that goes on in show business, and he capitalizes on it munificently. He's as easy to read as always, but you do have to be wary of the many hairpin curves of "coincidence" his plot is paved with. Even so, the killer is easily spotted. (C plus)*

Christopher Hale. *Murder on Display*. Doubleday (Crime Club), 1939, 280 pp.

Between the years 1935 and 1949 Christopher Hale, who apparently in real life was Frances Moyer Ross Stevens, had published a total of 13 mystery novels, 12 of them the detective adventures of Lt. Bill French of the State Homicide Squad. The state in question is Michigan, and Serena, the scene of this crime, is very much typical of the many small, lazy country towns found in the southern part of the state. Forty years ago or now, 50 miles from Detroit is the same as 500 miles away.

French is called in when the town's leading gossip is found strangled to death in the display window of Penbury's department store. Some anonymous notes from her hand come to light, but everyone's finger points French to the mysterious tramp blamed also for a recent attack on one of Serena's leading citizens.

There are lots of other clues, and French's chore is to pick out from the clutter the ones that will lead him to the killer. And, wow, it has been a while since I've read a story in which someone is kidnapped in an old Model T with the side curtains flapping!

French himself comes from a rich family dating from the state's glory days in lumbering. Not overwhelming in personality, he overcomes an initial impression of dilettantism (no, I didn't make up the word) to become a fairly competent detective. The stronger characterizations, however, belong to all the typically bucolic (in the non-offensive sense of the word) townspeople of Serena. (C)

John Evans. *Halo for Satan.* Bobbs-Merrill, 1948; 214 pp.

Chicago is a city with a hangover, a memento of its past. It's the city of Al Capone, of Louis Antuni, of Paul Pine, private eye. A wisecracking Dick Powell, I think, would fit the part perfectly. Pine doesn't make much money, he has a semi-sweet, sometimes sour, relationship with Homicide, but he is reliable and he is honest. Enough so that his services are called upon by His Grace, Bishop McManus, also of Chicago. He's asked to help reclaim a manuscript that's said to have been written by Jesus Christ himself.

This book is over thirty years old, but twenty-five million dollars is still plenty of money today. That's how much is at stake. You must realize that the Bishop is not the only person wanting his or her hands on the manuscript. There are, of course, a couple of women involved, but Evans' style is closer to that of Chandler than of Spillane. Neither Miss Lola North nor Mrs. Constance Benbrook are quite what they seem, but Mrs. B's agressive sexiness is less overtly believable. She is too blunt by far as to what she is, as a person or woman or wife.

Mix well and serve chilled. Ersatz Chandler and/or Hammett is bether than no ersatz at all. (B)

# VERDICTS

## (More Reviews)

Trevor Bernard. *Brightlight*. Manor, 1977, 204 pp.

I seem to have read a lot of p.i. novels lately. A few gradeAs—Parker, Bergman, Yuill; some grade Bs—Simon, Higgins, Lewin; an occasional C—Lewis Padgett; and below grade C (and there have been enough of them) I try not to read.
So where does new author Bernard and his oddly named detective, Nathan Brightlight, fit in? If the blurb were to be believed, "Hammett, Spillane, Chandler" (surely strange enough bedfellows in themselves) "and now Bernard ..." there could only be one answer. Well, the scenic descriptions are good, the characterizations reasonable for a 200 page paperback, and Brightlight himself is sharp enough in his repartee (though by no means a Spenser or a Hazell).
So by process of elimination it can only be the plot that leads me to award a grade B marking. A plot that has Brightlight called in to investigate the disappearance of the wife of a famous matinee idol. The trail leads to the idol's agent, to a former husband, a film starlet, a lush, a hophead, and a few more bit parts for good measure. And our man? Well, he beds a couple of women, gets involved in a shooting, and finally finds the wife and nails the killer. Not quite the brightest p.i. on the lot because I was ahead of him myself a couple of times; and sometimes his figuring left me a bit unhappy. "New" p.i. plots are virtually unfindable, but this one is just a little too reminiscent of some of the old favorites for comfort.
It wouldn't be fair to end without a mention of Brightlight's most endearing quality, his powers of introspection. So all in all a promising debut and the author should not be discouraged from trying his hand once more. (Bob Adey)

Curt Clark. *Anarchaos*. Ace, 1967, 143 pp.

*Anarchaos* is a science fiction adventure. It's also a mystery. You may think you've read something like it before. Rolfe Malone goes to the planet of Anarchaos, where there are no laws and no government and where survival of the fittest is the rule, to avenge the death of his brother. His intention is to discover who killed his brother and kill the killer, as simple as that. He believes that he is mean and keen and sharp. He's wrong. Almost before he knows it, he's been shot, beaten, and enslaved. Of course he does escape his enslavement, and of course he does find out tho killed his brother, but his final revenge is still something unique in this kind of venture. It's also oddly satisfying. The story has overtones of *The Count of Monte Cristo*, and the hero may remind you of Gully Foyle, but what Rolfe Malone goes through makes him different; and the depths to which he sinks make him almost pitiable. This is a good book for someone looking for something a little different. (Bill Crider)

Giles Tippette. *Wilson's Gold*. Dell, 1980, 224 pp., $1.50.

*Wilson's Gold* is a western.  It's also a caper novel.
Wilson Young, back from Tippette's excellent *The Bank Robber*,
is down on his luck and out of money.  He meets Chauncey Jones
by accident in a saloon, and Jones recognizes him from pictures on the wanted posters.  It seems that Jones has a foolproof plan for robbing a train, a plan so simple that it can
be executed by two men.  It's not of course.  Jones is too
young, naive, and talkative.  People show up where they're
not supposed to be.  Bullets don't go where they should.
People die.  Wilson survives, but just barely, and you can bet
that he doesn't live happily ever after.  Tippette is quite a
storyteller, and if you don't mind your caper novels set 100
years in the past, you could do worse than *Wilson's Gold*.
(Bill Crider)

Bill Pronzini. *Labyrinth*. St. Martin's Press, 1980, 186 pp.,
   $8.95.

 He is the last pulpster.  Those lurid-covered old magazines like *Black Mask, Detective Fiction Weekly* and *Dime Detective*, which spawned Dashiell Hammett and Raymond Chandler
and dozens of other talents and revolutionized American crime
fiction, are central to San Francisco mystery writer Bill
Pronzini's life and work in a variety of ways.  He has read
and collected pulps avidly for years.  Like the great pulpsters, he is tirelessly prolific behind the typewriter, turning out work in a multitude of genres—mysteries, science
fiction, westerns, spicy stories—by himself and with a number
of collaborators, under his own name, joint bylines, pseudonyms and house names.  His most famous series character, a
nameless San Francisco private detective, not only is a pulp
collector like his creator, but often thinks of himself as a
figment of a pulp writer's imagination, and occasionally
solves a case thanks to recalling some detail of a pulp story
he has read.

 *Labyrinth*, which is Pronzini's eighteenth novel and the
sixth book-length adventure of the nameless private eye, deals
with three separate cases—the murder of a young woman near
Lake Merced, the psychological torment of a guilt-ridden man
who seeks punishment for a fatal auto accident in which he was
involved, and the disappearance of a budding young investigative reporter in the northern California fishing village of
Bodega Bay.  Like countless earlier pulp writers who eventually turned to book-length mystery fiction, Pronzini has constructed this book as well as several others out of his own
previously published short stories, expanding, deleting,
changing and combining characters and plot elements as needed.*
Unhappily, the connective tissue among the three cases turns
out to be, in the detective's own words, "a crazy-quilt of
coincidence."  *Labyrinth* is by no means Pronzini's best but
it's a solidly readable job, graced by one or two neat clues
and some vivid evocations of San Francisco and points north,
demonstrating that the story-telling skills which the great
pulp writers bequeathed to subsequent generations are alive

---

*The three source stories all come from *Alfred Hitchcock's Mystery Magazine*: "A Cold Day in November" (November 1969), "The Way the World Spins" (May 1970), and "The Scales of Justice" (July 1973).

and well in the shadow of the Golden Gate. (Francis M. Nevins, Jr.)

LeRoy Panek. *Watteau's Shepherds: The Detective Novel in Britain, 1914-1940.* Bowling Green University Popular Press, 1979, 232 pp., $13.95 hardback, $5.95 paperback.

The classic formal detective novel flourished in England and the United States roughly from the end of the first World War to the beginning of the Second. The murder victims in these novels never bled, the survivors never mourned; in fact, as Robert Graves once remarked, detective novels had no more to do with the real world of crime and punishment than Watteau's paintings of idealized shepherds had to do with the realities of sheep-raising. But the best of those novels generated a unique intellectual excitement that combined the thrill of the chase, the challenge of an elaborate but scrupulously fair game of wits, and the meaningfulness of a quest for truth, albeit the narrowly circumscribed truth as to Who Done It.

This type of book survives and remains quite popular today, as witness the perpetual reprinting of Agatha Christie, Dorothy L. Sayers and Ellery Queen. But what makes the detective novel tick? The innards of the genre have been examined minutely by all sorts of scholars, most recently by LeRoy Panek of Western Maryland College, who discusses the Golden Age of British detective fiction in terms of (1) intellectual reaction against the wild hair's-breadth thrillers that dominated popular fiction in England during the Nineteen Teens; (2) the need of certain cultivated writers and readers for a kind of fiction rooted in labyrinthine intellectual play; (3) a later reaction of writers with mainstream literary aims against the bloodless artificiality of the "pure" puzzle novel. At the heart of Panek's book is a series of detailed analyses of eight Golden Age novelists (including Christie, Sayers, John Dickson Carr and Ngaio March) which display a firm grasp on each writer's individual contributions while working within a fixed yet flexible tradition.

Professor of English though he is, Panek demonstrably loves those great old puzzles, and his enthusiasm lends a joyous readability, marred only by a plague of misspelled proper names, to what could easily have been a deadly ponderous tome. Even the Appendix in which he uses a flow chart to diagram the genre's internal operations is as delightful as it is instructive. Here is a book about mystery fiction which combines scholarship and good humor without elitism or cutesiness--an achievement as rare as a perfect detective novel. (Francis M. Nevins, Jr.)

Barry Perowne. *Raffles of the Albany: Footprints of a Famous Gentleman Crook in the Times of a Great Detective.* St. Martin's, 1976, 212 pp.

This is the second collection of Raffles pastiches, from EQMM and *The Saint Magazine*. By now, the formula has been set: Raffles goes to an exotic locale, meets a character ripped from the pages of history, encounters something/somebody worth stealing, always making sure that the theft is for good persons wronged by bad persons, engages in the heist, and makes

sure that the good people live happily ever after—with, of
course, Raffles getting his share of the swag. These are competent stories, enlightened by an acerbic wit, but quite forgettable. Undemanding Victoriana. (B) (Martin Morse Wooster)

Geoffrey Household. *The Courtesy of Death*. Atlantic/Little,
   Brown, 1967, 214 pp.

Geoffrey Household is the most prominent example of a
suspense writer who has endured by rewriting his first novel.
That novel, *Rogue Male*, is a classic, and well worth reading;
its successors have had varying degrees of quality.

In this rewrite of *Rogue Male* the hero, a retired engineer,
accidentally encounters a crew of sinister cultists who believe in an obscure fertility religion, updated to suit the
tenor of the 1960s. Our hero is kidnapped, hides in a cave
for two weeks, discovers the real motives of the cultists,
and, as in so many Household novels, goes bounding across the
moors pursued by the police and the religiosos. A gimcrack
plot, a tawdry religion, and dimbulb characterd do not help
matters. The worst Household novel I've read. (C-) (Martin
Morse Wooster)

Isaac Asimov, Martin Harry Greenberg, and Charles Waugh, eds.
   *The Thirteen Crimes of Science Fiction*. Doubleday, 1979,
   455 pp.

Martin Harry Greenberg and Charles Waugh are two leaders
of a combine that churns out anthologies of science fiction
and fantasy in vast profusion. They have edited, with various
partners, two anthologies of importance to mystery fans: *Mysterious Visions* (St. Martin's, 1979), being stories of the
fantastic by mystery writers, and this volume, mystery tales
by science fiction writers.

Although I understand that not every story in here was the
first choice of the editors, they have managed to compile a
fine anthology. Included are hard-boiled sf novellas by Tom
Reamy ("The Detweiler Boy") and Larry Niven ("ARM"); stories
with analytic detectives by Isaac Asimov, Randall Garrett, and
Avram Davidson; and crackpot comedy in the Donald Westlake
manner by Clifford Simak. All of these stories are mysteries
in one sense or another; and half the book is comprised of
brilliant stories (namely those by Reamy, Garrett, Philip K.
Dick, Asimov, Niven, Simak, and William Tenn). The other
half range from competent to blasé; only the tales of Edward
Wellen and William F. Temple tell are outright turkeys. A
good collection well worth the $12.50 for the hardcover, and
a definite buy in paperback. (A-) (Martin Morse Wooster)

Stephen King. *Night Shift*. Doubleday, 1978, 336 pp.

One of the more interesting phenomena of the seventies is
that developments in the mystery short story have, for the
most part, not taken place within the field. The short suspense tale has been developed by "outsiders"—writers such as
Robert Aickman and Ramsey Campbell that are not normally recognized as writing suspense fiction but are, instead, catalogued as "horror" writers. But the dichotomy between the
macabre and the mysterious is not that exact—witness the suc-

cess of the Alfred Hitchcock anthologies.

Stephen King is catalogued as a "horror" writer by many, and, indeed, his latest short fictions have tended to be more fantasy than mystery. But the stories collected in *Night Shift* are of much more concern to our field; their emphasis is on the discovery of the object from beyond rather than descriptions of the object itself. All but one of these stories are contemporary, and all display a far keener sense of the currents of American popular culture than all EQMM writers of the past five years, with the exceptions of David Ely, Patricia Highsmith, and Robert Bloch. Highly recommended. (A) (Martin Morse Wooster)

Donald Hamilton. *The Intriguers*. Fawcett, 1972, 208 pp.

The fourteenth Matt Helm thriller puts this series into new directions. When Helm goes on vacation in Mexico he is shot at by sinister forces. He quickly discovers that these sinister forces are controlled by Herbert Leonard, who is trying to unite all the U.S. intelligence services into a single unit under his command. Leonard is busily wiping out all those spies who oppose him, including Mac's entire unit; thus armed with power, and allied with a powerful feminist/pacifist presidential candidate, Leonard hopes to control America....

This could have been one of the more powerful of the Helm books. Hamilton, trying to work himself out of a rut, errs too far on the side of unbelievability; too many characters spend too much time musing about the Meaning of It All. Hamilton is trying to move from the fantasized formulaic fiction of his earlier novels into a tougher and more brutal style. *The Intriguers* marks the beginning of the change from external to internal threats; one hopes that a "new" and more fully developed Helm will emerge in the next four novels. (B-) (Martin Mores Wooster)

# THE DOCUMENTS IN THE CASE
## (Letters)

From Karen LaPorte, 1546 Silver St., Hermosa Beach, CA 90254:
TMF arrived last night and, as usual, I enjoyed reading it especially Mysteriously Speaking. Your employer sounds like most of the "idiots" one has to deal with in advertising. The following is for David Doerrer who commented about my catalog on Page 46.
  1) The Green Ripper may still be available in Florida at the publisher's price but Florida isn't California. And furthermore ... looking back at the amount of books that I have sold in Florida last year (books that aren't difficult to get) it seems to me that there aren't that many bookstores around.
  2) I took a $9.95 book and put it in my catalogue for $13.50. Well that isn't much of a markup. I got one in the mail last night which still had the price in it (they either forgot of didn't bother). The price marked was 50¢. I paid $7.50 for it. Now that's a markup.
  3) Evidently Mr. Doerrer didn't notice (and I doubt if he would since he hasn't bought anything out of either catalogue) that I include both postage & insurance on every book that I sell. And *nobody* (I state that emphatically) does that anymore. Even if you buy a $25.00 book you still end up paying additional for postage and insurance. I do not state (like everyone else in the beginning of their lists or catalogues) that "I am not responsible for uninsured packages". When I sell a book I am responsible for its delivery whether it be the Post Office (which I trust like "a hole in the head") or United Parcel (which is a lot better). Every book that I sell (be it $6.00 or $35.00) is securely wrapped in brown paper and packaged in a padded bag. And if you think that I get these items for nothing ... you've got another "think" coming. It costs me an average (and I state average) of $1.75 to ship a book including postage, insurance, mailing bag & wrapping paper. And don't think that this isn't built into the price of the book because it is.
  4) My catalogue [*to be honest, Karen spelled the word g-u-e in the first paragraph above, but I dropped off the u-e since the word came at the end of a line and I didn't have room. Just didn't want you folks to think she was inconsistent.*] may be a list to Mr. Doerrer and if it looked like half the ones I receive in the mail I could print it a good deal cheaper than I do. It costs me approximately $1.50 (including printing, postage & advertising) to mail one catalogue. And this doesn't include my own labor (or even the gas which is now at $1.35 a gallon out here) in finding the books, cleaning them up or cataloguing them. In two catalogues of over 500 books I've only had two returns and they weren't from inaccuracy of description or condition. Now that's not a bad percentage.
  5) Another comment he made was "seems to have a good selection". Now really, isn't that a matter of taste? Or as the old cliche goes "One Man's Meat is another man's poison". In book hunting (I'm probably stating a fact that everyone knows but I'll do it anyway) it all depends on what you can find at what price ... what's the condition ... do you really

want to sell it or keep it in your own collection and on and on. There is a good selection in my catalogue. There are some items (especially the R. T. Campbell's and the Joseph Show) that I have rarely seen in others.

6) And finally ... as one gets older one gets a little wiser (hopefully). The books in my first catalogue were priced much too low. You learn that in a hurry when another dealer buys it from you and then puts it in his catalogue at three times the price you sold it to him for.

So, Mr. Doerrer, be a little more polite in your comments next time. Or better, perhaps, get all the facts first. Incidentally, The Green Ripper was sold the first week the catalogue was mailed. And the man that brought it lives in Florida.

Guy, if all the above sounds a bit "snotty" it's the way I felt when I read his comments. But go ahead and print it anyway. [*Okay.*]

From Linda Toole, 147 Somershire Dr., Rochester, NY 14617:

TMF is ruining my life! Monday I was going to bed (1:0.0 a.m.) and stopped to check *one* map on a Dell Mapback. On my way out of the room, I saw the stack of TMF's that I've been slowly working my way through. I succumbed, and the next thing I knew the birds were singing, the sun was rising, and it was 5:00 a.m.! A bit tough when you have to go to work that day. It was, however, time well spent.

Since many TMFers enjoy Nero Wolfe, I thought you might be interested in a brief note of what occurred at the recent Wolfe Pack event (4/24) "A Shad Roe Dinner". Obviously, the major attraction was the opportunity to sample one of Wolfe's favorite dishes--Shad Roe. Ours was Shad Roe Aux Fines Herbes (from *The Nero Wolfe Cookbook,* of course). I approached the meal with a certain amount of trepidation. I had never tried it before, but felt obligated to in view of the prominent (culinary) part it plays in many of the N.W. stories. I'm happy to report that I did enjoy it.

One feature of the evening was a contest, "How Many Roe in a Pair of Shad Roe?" The Authority was Dr. Isaac Asimov, the prize an autographed copy of his second Black Widowers' book, and the correct answer 486,000. Several songs on Shad Roe were composed and sung. The most memorable being, "The Shad Roe of Your Smile". Unfortunately, I don't have a copy of the complete lyrics. Everyone was also asked to write a limerick on the Saga and/or Shad Roe. Dr. Asimov then read aloud all the contributions to much cheering and occasional groans. A thoroughly delightful evening with good people. Rather like an evening with TMF.

Since Mr. Loeser is "retiring", perhaps you might like to take over the title of Curmudgeon. [*Who, me?*] Your frequent railings against unreadable copy almost made me retype the first page (even though I had corrected the typos). Whether or not this letter sees print, I hope you appreciate the fact that it is double-speced and typed! [*I do, indeed.*]

From Bob Adey, 7 Highcroft Ave., Wordsley, Stourbridge, West Midlands, DY8 5LX, England:

Sincere apologies for having been a pretty lousy correspondent over recent matters.

I have been receiving *Fancier* with the usual delight and

reading with the usual pleasure, but not finding the time and inclination to write in. However, the silence is now broken.

And what news have I? Frankly not a hell of a lot. News that Peter Lovesey's novels are being televised on the commercial channel (one hour long book per week for seven weeks) but I can't review 'em, because I ain't watchin' 'em—and I ain't watchin' 'em because I want to read them (if you follow me [*I do, indeed, since I have the same reluctance to watch a movie or televised version of a book I eventually intend to read but have not yet gotten around to; Incidentally, you won't have this problem next year as I understand Lovesey is now at work writing original screen plays for half a dozen or so episoces of Sergeant Cribb et cie—since they will be original you can watch them without feeling guilty. Since I have read all but one or two of the Lovesey books, including the ones that were shown in this country, I was able to view them all with great enjoyment. I thought* Wobble to Death *and* Swing, Swing Together *were extremely good, but* Abracadaver *was embarrassingly weak.*]). Newspaper reviews have been quite favorable.

A tip also that more paperback original short story (TV spin-off) collections have been published over here. Two 6 story Rumpole books by John Mortimer (published by Penguin) and the Enigma Files by Christine Sparks. This is a current BBC TV series, and the book is published simultaneously in hardback and paperback. [*Several episodes of the Rumpole series were shown in this country this past year, and I don't hesitate for a moment to call them the best TV fare I've seen in a long, long time.*]

From Fred Dueren, 2409 Oakwood Blvd., Wausau, WI 54401:

I've been slow in getting this letter off to you. I'd intended to read all the back copies and throw in my comments all at once. But between having too many other things to read and wanting to space out *The MYSTERY FANcier* so it would be enjoyed longer, I thought I'd better write now on what I have to say.

Obviously I enjoy TMF immensely and hope that as any other publishing problems come up you are able to resolve them. I like the blend of material presented and openess of opinion from the readers. It is encouraging to know that many others get as frustrated as I do at the impossibility of reading everything that sounds good or interesting in some way. Reading TMF and other mystery fanzines has sharpened my desire to write a few more articles myself. This letter is kind of my first step. All I have to do is keep the ambition going.
[*We TMFers impatiently await the articles, Fred; it's been too long since you were heard from.*]

In Volume 2, No. 4 David Doerrer asked if there was any interest in a reprinting of checklists. YES!! If it is not covered in one of the later issues and has dropped, I'll be disappointed. If David's still working on it and needs help I can give some minimal assistance (I think).

I have not seen it mentioned anywhere yet so I wonder if many of the subscribers are aware of *Twentieth-Century Crime and Mystery Writers* to be published later this year by St. Martin's Press. The actual publishing date has not been announced yet as far as I know [*See Mysteriously Speaking...*]. It will have biographies, comments by, critical essays of and bibliographies of all the major crime writers.

Dell Books has announced a new series of mysteries to be published starting in September. Actually two series—"Murder Ink" and "Scene of the Crime". The proprietresses of those two stores have chosen which books to publish and will have their name and logo on the cover. The choices are to be books that have never been published in the U.S. or classics that are out of print. The first four announced are Sheila Radley's *Death in the Morning* [*hold on there, Fred—Death in the Morning was published in the U.S. last year by Scribner's, so their criteria must be a bit more flexible than you say*], Pauline Glen Winslow's *The Brandenburg Hotel*, Robert Barnard's *Death of a Mystery Writer*, and Mignon Warner's *A Medium for Murder*.

Also in the line of new books to watch for, Harlequin Books (of the romance fame) is bring out original paperback mysteries under Raven House Mysteries imprint. The authors of the first four books in that line are unknown to me, but it is good to see the "mystery" come back into publication instead of all the suspense and occult books. At least the advance notices make them sound like detective/mystery fare.

From Bill Crider, 4206 Ninth Street, Brownwood, TX 76801:

I have to say that it was quite a relief to see Steve Lewis back with us in TMF 4, 2. I was afraid for a while there that he might have forgotten to renew. I don't think I could face life without his reviews.

Jeff Banks's article and chart were excellent, and his homage to Modesty was long overdue [*Overdue in more ways than one, since I had it on hand for a year or better before using it, which made it out of date before it saw print; then I had to compound my guilt by laying out the pages wrong—they were supposed to be* facing *pages....*]. I'm not sure just why O'Donnell hasn't received much attention, but the material provided in the article was a good start. I do wish a bibliography giving publishing information could have been added. I've only been able to find two (I think) of the Modesty books in paperback, and I'd like to know if others have been published in that format.

www.ingramcontent.com/pod-product-compliance
Lightning Source LLC
Chambersburg PA
CBHW031308060426
42444CB00032B/810